THE JOHN WESLEY
Prayer Book

•

COMMENTARY BY

W. MAYNARD FRENCH

•

THE PARTHENON PRESS
Nashville Tennessee

Foreword

THERE IS A NEW LOOK IN METHODISM, and not only in Methodism, but in many of the larger Protestant denominations. This new look is in effect the "dressing-up" of our clergy, church buildings, and worship services. Its widening influence prompts a Baptist to write, "How little most people who attend religious services each Sunday comprehend of the governing principles of their observance, and how much less do the people who stay away from churches appreciate the profound and lasting values in the religious ceremonial!"

This new look, or as it is called by many the "liturgical movement," prompted in 1948 under the direction of the General Council of the Congregational Christian Churches in the United States that *A Book of Worship for Free Churches* be published in which were foreworded these words: "When, to the lifting up of our own innermost needs and hopes, we add the beloved and timetested prayers and the common worship of the innumerable company who have gone on before us, our worship takes on depth and beauty."

Recently the movement prompted the publication of *Christian Worship: A Service Book,* by a Disciple professor at Phillip's University. Added to this is a list of many volumes, pamphlets, and articles which of late have been compiled and printed in the field of worship and symbolism.

In 1940 our own denomination appointed a Commission on Ritual and Orders of Worship which four years later issued *The Book of Worship for Church and Home.*

In many areas this new look has not been confined to commissions or an occasional author but has trickled down to the local church. It is not uncommon to hear congregations responding more and more frequently in worship services. The pattern of worship itself is more formal and fixed. The minister may be appearing more often in stole and clerical collar with vested choir flanking him on either side of the chancel. The chancel itself bespeaks the new look. Center pulpits are deferring to pulpit and lectern arrangements with altar placed against the front wall of the sanctuary.

Increasing evidence strongly suggests that for many years to come the Free Churches will be involved in the waxing and waning phases of a liturgical movement. Incidentally, the Roman Catholic Church is also confronted with a liturgical movement of different sorts. In the Roman Church the movement purposes a simplification of rites and ceremonies. It may be a belated reflection upon Augustine's fifty-fifth epistle in which he laments to Januarius that a variety of artificial and burdensome usages had been growing up around the few simple sacraments of the church, until now he complains "the Christians are as perplexed as Jews over the multiplicity of rites and ceremonies."

While "Methodism has never been considered a liturgical church . . ." as *The Book of Worship* rightly insists, we have liturgical parents in the Church of England and before that the Roman Catholic Church. This fact in itself means little, however, without a well-founded desire by each local congregation to explore with their minister the possibilities of meaningful liturgical worship. Perhaps that desire can be pregnable if the congregation is armed with an explanation of the liturgical drama being unraveled before their eyes each Sunday.

ARCHITECTURE

Congregations who do not know the difference between a Te Deum and a missal stand are enthusiastically supporting the Board of Home Missions and Church Extension's insistence that new churches include a chancel and center aisle. This may not be totally reflective of a growing concern for liturgical use. It often merely appeals to an aesthetic appreciation of beauty and form, the tastefully appointed altar framed by an artistic reredos being more attractive than a pulpit incased by variagated choir chairs.

This may be a valid reason for a chancel arrangement. The minister who preaches against a background of mobile choir faces must struggle for undivided attention. A yawning, giggling, or bored face can easily destroy the effectiveness of a well-prepared sermon.

Historically the altar has been the center of focus. An altar is the progeny of sacrifice and therefore is an indigenous part of any religion which implies a sacrificial nature. Christ upon the Cross can leave little doubt that Christianity from the beginning has been a sacrificial religion. The Cross upon the altar reminds us that we are still challenged to make deep and lasting sacrifices in a day of selfishness and a society characterized by greed and gluttony.

It is an interesting, although incongruous, phenomenon to visit churches where each church school classroom has a small altar or table with cross and candles but the sanctuary is defunct of any symbol of our Lord's sacrifice for mankind. One choir sensitive to this situation sang in a processional:

> Onward, Christian soldiers,
> Marching as to war,
> With the Cross of Jesus
> Hid behind the door.

Since the altar rightly has the position of importance the pulpit and lectern are moved to the side. Tradition places the pulpit to the left of the altar. On whichever side it is placed, however, it should suggest strength and dignity. Here are uttered the prophetic words of truth. These words of truth and Biblical exposition in the Protestant church are important to man's salvation. Therefore, in a very practical sense the pulpit is set apart from flickering altar candles, choir, organist, or other objects which might distract attention from the sermon.

Similarly the lectern, smaller than the pulpit, with the Bible open upon it has a place of its own. The lectern symbolizes the veneration given to the Holy Scriptures throughout the ages. (There are many manuals for altar guilds which explain the symbolism of coverings and antependia for altar, pulpit, and lectern.)

VESTMENTS

Vestments for clergy, choir, and acolytes are becoming increasingly popular. The simplest vestment is the robe. For years choirs have seen the practical implications of covering the multicolored dresses, suits, and ties with the simplicity of a robe. This it seems to me is reason enough for choir robes.

The vested clergyman divorces himself from the idiosyncrasy of gaudy or ostentatious dress. He speaks as a prophet-priest of the Lord, not as the charcoal-gray-suited man of the street. To emphasize this prophetic preaching position some ministers wear a stole which is the ancient symbol of "the yoke of Jesus," or of the preaching ministry, in contrast to the ministries of healing or music. Using this definition it is improper for choirs to appear in stoles of any kind.

Some Methodist ministers wear a white surplice over a black cassock. Originally the white surplice was used for baptisms and may be used in any Protestant denomination.

The clerical collar is a part of the new look. George Hedley in his book, *Christian Worship,* gives this reasoning for the wearing of the clerical collar: "One does not become less validly human when he has the collar on, though indeed he may be inclined to behave better than he might when hidden in the anonymity of a red tie or an aloha shirt. With the collar he does become a visible, living reminder that some men have given themselves wholly to God, and that they are not ashamed of their high calling in Christ Jesus."

Those reasons which insist upon choir and clergy to be vested would hold true for acolytes or servers. While a janitor can light candles as efficiently as a young boy there is a certain unmistakable dignity to the act when done by the vested acolyte during a procession.

WORSHIP

The service of worship is usually the last ramification of the new look to be paraded before the congregation. Oftentimes it is also the least understood.

Morning worship in most Protestant churches follows more or less the ancient Morning Prayer from the Canonical Hours. (The Protestant Episcopal Church follows it much more while the Pentecostal groups follow it much less.) But there is a basic pattern.

The pattern for Morning Prayer is outlined in Isaiah 6:1-9. Isaiah's worship experience is the experience of real worship. It has been formalized into an order of worship that all might share in the prophet's joy. Read the account carefully. Isaiah's first words are those of praise to the holiness of God. Isaiah's second thought was his unworthiness in the sight of God in all his glory. This prompted him to confess and that moved God to forgive. The goodness and mercy of God lead Isaiah to dedicate his life to him.

This is in essence what should take place in worship. A hymn to the glory of God; a deep feeling of unworthiness voiced corporately in a general prayer of confession; the assurance of forgiveness pronounced by the minister; the affirmation of our faith by Psalter, creed, and lessons; and then arrival at the same conclusion that Isaiah reached, that we must not leave this hallowed place until we rededicate our lives to God.

Any service which does not lead in this direction is not worship in its best sense. Homemade services may be filled with responses, bowing and scrapings, chanting and litanies, beautifully vested actors, and liturgically appointed and fitted sanctuaries—but without this basic pattern leading to the dedication of life, or as the Methodists call it "an invitation to Christian discipleship," the service has not been an experience of worship.

Having now said this much the purpose of this book should be clear. No minister or congregation should take upon themselves the architectural settings, vestments, or worship that bespeaks a liturgical approach to religion without study, prayer, and much explaining. *The John Wesley Prayer Book* may help to define the climate of our two major worship services, Holy Communion and Morning Prayer. By its arrangement the machinery of worship has been cut to a minimum. Choir, clergy, and congregation can follow Holy Communion as it progresses without scrambling for responses, creeds, or music since all the Communion ingredients follow in order. By the use of its prefaces to each service study groups may be formed to explore the background and meaning of Holy Communion and Morning and Evening Prayer for an enriched worship experience.

It is said that Thomas Cranmer compiled the first English Prayer Book that there might again be an orderly recitation of the Scriptures. Certainly one of the reasons for a book of this nature is to promote an orderly and intelligent recitation of the liturgy. St. Paul reminds us: "For God is not a God of confusion but of peace." (I Cor. 14:33*a*.)

Contents

MORNING PRAYER

MORNING PRAYER

FOR A MILLENNIUM AND A HALF the Sunday morning worship in Christian churches was the celebration of the Mass. Through revisions and additions from time to time, the Mass had by the early sixteenth century become a complete expression of Christian worship.

The German reformers of that century were aware of the perfect objectivity of the Eucharist and altered only the language in which it was spoken when accepting it *in toto* for their Sunday worship.

While the Mass was accepted in England as the basis for Sunday worship, a problem arose with the publication of the first *Book of Common Prayer* in 1549 by Thomas Cranmer. Mattins was called Morning Prayer and the Mass was called Holy Communion. The reformers and writers of the Prayer Book did not intend that Morning Prayer should be an alternative to Holy Communion.

A rubric, however, stated that Communion could not be administered without proper notice a week before and that the curate must list those who would be present. If there was an insufficient numbei signed up there would be no communion.

Often there were not enough signatories in advance and as a result Holy Communion was not celebrated. Inadvertently this led to the use of the more popular Morning Prayer as the standard for Sunday worship.

John Wesley used the service of Morning Prayer as did all priests of his time. And while Wesley urged that communion be celebrated at least once a week, he continued to follow the accepted pattern of Morning Prayer for Sunday worship.

It was only natural, therefore, that in 1784 he should prepare for the societies in America a service similar to that of Morning Prayer.

He added a note of authority to the preface by writing: "I believe there is no Liturgy in the World, either in ancient or modern language, which breathes more of a solid, scriptural, rational Piety, than the Common Prayer of the Church of England. And though the main of it was compiled considerable more than two hundred years ago, yet is the language of it, not only pure, but strong and elegant in the highest degree."

The Sunday Service that Wesley prepared for the American

societies never became popular in America. There were many reasons for its disuse. The austerity of colonial New England infected the religious practices of many faiths and caused a basic distrust for liturgy. On the wilderness boundaries the vociferous nature of frontier life was not compatible with the formal beauty of the Sunday Service.

The greatest deterrent to its use, however, was that it was impractical. Liturgy insists on response and setting, neither of which were possible in frontier areas. Even the Anglican Church in the Colonies found it difficult to read Morning Prayer with a shortage of Prayer Books. The Methodist, without sufficient copies of the Sunday Service and with only sail lofts in which to meet, had neither setting nor occasion for response.

Today many ministers have the architectural setting for Wesley's service. Every minister and congregation has access to the service since it has been included as an optional order of worship in the Hymnal.

Perhaps with a less foggy vision of the movement, with its various moods and tones, the service can again be to us the means of grace that it was for Wesley. At worst it is a worthy substitute for occasional use; at best it is a complete expression of our total dependence upon God.

The present order for Morning or Evening Prayer as it appears in paragraph 1906 of the 1952 Discipline is an adaptation of John Wesley's Sunday Service for the Methodists of North America, which was itself an adaptation of the Daily Office of Morning Prayer from the English Book of Common Prayer.

The style of the English office dates back to Archbishop Cranmer who constructed the order of Morning Prayer from the ancient offices of the Church—Lauds, Mattins, and Prime. His purpose in restoring the ancient offices was to present again an orderly recitation of the Scriptures.

It was this service which Wesley knew and loved as the typical Sunday worship. Our order for Morning Prayer is similar in mood to the office of Wesley's time. This English office, with only a few changes and deletions, is a prototype of the Order for Daily Morning Prayer in the American Book of Common Prayer.

The service begins with the rubric: "Let the service of worship begin at the time appointed. Let the people kneel or bow in silent prayer upon entering the sanctuary."

The attitude of worship is not achieved entirely by the mechanical bowing or kneeling of the worshiper upon entering the sanctuary. The hoped for effect and justification of enforced silent prayer is that it will start the individual in the worship experience by concentration on the majesty of God and his own unworthiness before him.

This is being done presumably during the prelude. Yet even in the case of late-comers, kneeling, where possible, and silent prayer should precede any attempt to integrate oneself into the current phase of the worship.

The Scripture sentences serve in place of an introit, setting the theme and mood of the entire service. The majority of the sentences are penitential in mood, conditioning the congregation for the Call to Confession.

A processional hymn may precede or follow the sentences. In either case a hymn of adoration is out of context with the general mood of contrition before God.

In the earlier offices the hymn came later in the service after the pronouncement of absolution by the priest. There are several processional hymns, however, that can be used at this juncture which at least allude to the penitential mood. (Third stanza, "Nicaea," ". . . Though the eye of sinful man . . .")

The sentences prepare the worshiper for the exhortation, when, being moved by the Scriptures, he is called upon to confess his sins. Isaiah 6:1-8 dramatically suggests that there can be no communion with God until a declaration of man's disobedience has been made and reconciliation sought.

In the Episcopal service the Call to Confession is longer and outlines more of the elements of corporate worship. The adapted order from Wesley's Sunday Service stops with the need for repentance, especially when we come together to give thanks to God for all his gifts and mercies to unworthy recipients.

The General Confession is to be said by all while in the posture of prayer. It is unfortunate that so few Methodist churches have the proper fixtures to comply with the rubric which suggests kneeling.

Kneeling imposes not only the attitude of humility of body but also of mind, one augmenting the other.

The General Confession is second only to the Lord's Prayer in importance. It is inadvisable to omit it consistently from the Sunday morning service as do some leaders of worship. Such a practice denies the individual in the congregation the opportunity to join with others in a confession of sin which is vital to worship.

The confession is a fabric of scriptural sentences woven into a complete pattern of contrition. The prayer is based on St. Paul's analysis of sin in Romans 7:8-25.

The General Confession "is a tissue of Biblical phrases that reminds us of our self assertions and the following of our own devices and desires instead of living for God." So says Massey H. Shepherd, Jr., in the *Oxford American Prayer Book Commentary.* Truly few prayers are more important for us today than this.

The Prayer of Pardon is not a declaration of absolution as it is in the Morning Prayer of the Episcopal Church. It is, as the name implies, a prayer for forgiveness. It is not to be construed as a pronouncement of forgiveness by the minister.

In the ancient offices only a bishop could pronounce absolution. Later, parish priests were allowed the privilege. Wesley, unwilling that an unordained minister pronounce absolution, sent to America a prayer suitable for use by his lay preachers. The prayer calls on God to forgive those who have so recently enumerated their sins.

While the writer does not presume to give a commentary on our Lord's Prayer, it is necessary to spell out one of its several meanings to show the intelligence of its placement after the Prayer for Pardon. Certainly one of the inferred meanings of the Lord's Prayer is the peace and inward calm that comes from a complete trust in God as a father. A father who supplies all our needs, one of which is forgiveness, is quite important to mental health. Therefore, it comes at an appropriate place and gives added support to the Prayer for Pardon.

With the conclusion of confession and forgiveness, Morning Prayer moves into a new mood, one of joy and praise. The first pair of versicles, a transcript of Psalm 51:15, introduces the coming pattern of praise.

No more simple statement can be made than this, as it directs the congregation to the jubilant *Venite:* "O Lord, open thou our lips. And our mouth shall show forth thy praise. Praise ye the Lord. The Lord's name be praised."

It is small wonder that this service can boast an uninterrupted history of at least four hundred years; its orderliness and connectional qualities defy disuse.

With the rehearsal of the versicles the worshiper stands and sings Psalm 95, the *Venite.* The *Venite* joyfully summons all creatures of the world to worship God, the Creator, Provider, and Judge, with praise and thanksgiving. It functions as a natural prelude to the reading of both the Psalm and the Lessons.

Those versions that include the last four verses, "To-day, if ye will hear his voice, harden not your heart . . . ," give the *Venite* more credence than the modernized forms as a vehicle for introducing the period of instruction.

The various Psalms that follow the *Venite* have a wide range in mood and context. They integrate two outstanding attitudes, however, that are necessary for worship. They mirror the Psalmist's complete sincerity and unfailing trust in God without which worship loses all meaning and becomes "as sounding brass, or a tinkling cymbal."

The reading of the Psalm always concludes with the *Gloria Patri.* This use is traditional, dating back to the earliest times, and is placed there to give the Psalms a Christian framework. It is inappropriate to sing the *Gloria Patri* after the *Venite* as it is suggested in the Book of Worship in this particular form of Worship.

The first lesson from the Old Testament begins the period of instruction. Unfortunately the lectionary in the Book of Worship has but eight Old Testament readings listed for the first lesson for the entire Christian year. It might be helpful to use the lectionary in the Book of Common Prayer for the first lesson.

The *Te Deum laudamus,* separating the Old and New Testament lessons, is one of the two great hymns of the Church, the other being the *Gloria in excelsis.*

Most congregations will find it easier to read the *Te Deum* instead of singing this non-scriptural canticle. Ideally the canticle should be sung since it takes the place of an anthem in Wesley's Sunday

Service. If it is not used a suitable anthem should be substituted for it.

The *Te Deum* is divided into three parts. The first part, verses 1-13, is a hymn to the Trinity. The second part, verses, 14-21, is a hymn to Christ. This parallels the Apostles' Creed and issues a succinct statement of what the church believes about the Son of God. Verse 21 is the climax to the hymn, with the third part a later addition which might well be omitted.

John Wesley included the *Te Deum* at this point because Cranmer in the 1552 Prayer Book used this form. It would be more logical and just as proper, however, if the *Benedictus* (Luke 1:68-80) was sung at this juncture. The Song of Zacharias is a perfect link between the Old and New Testaments. This canticle speaks of the Lord's forerunner, John the Baptist, which makes it better qualified to introduce the Gospel.

After the second lesson follows the *Jubilate Deo*. This hymn is an invitation to give thanks to the three eternal qualities of God: his mercy and loving kindness, his goodness, and his faithfulness. These distinct qualities are delimited more clearly in the Revised Standard Version than they are in Tyndale's translation from which the canticles in the Hymnal and Book of Worship are taken.

The mood of the *Jubilate Deo* moves the worshiper to declare his faith by reciting the Apostles' Creed. In the words of George Hedley, to omit the creed ". . . is to imply either that the church lacks a common faith, or that for some reason it is afraid to assert it."

The Apostles' Creed is the oldest statement of faith in continuous use in Christendom. Its use dated back to the middle of the second century.

Candidates for baptism first used the creed for instructional and declaratory purposes. Later additions were made to sharpen the distinctions of the Christian faith against that of the Marcionites and the Gnostics. There is nothing in the creed incongruous with the Scriptures.

The versicle that follows the creed, in a very practical sense, keeps the minds of the congregation from wandering. Many of the more informal services of worship allow by neglect the corporate mind of the worshiper to go afield at every change of mood or shift of emphasis. There is little opportunity in Wesley's Sunday Service for mind wanderings or lack of interest.

The prayers for Peace and Grace preclude a pastoral prayer. These two prayers in a very succinct fashion cover those petitions that are usually trampled upon by the verboseness of most pastoral prayers.

In the Collect for Peace, corporate acknowledgment is made to God for his continual love extended to us now and forever. We do not ask that sin and evil be removed from our sight but that, living in the world of sin, we might be given power to overcome it.

The Collect for Grace is similar to the preceding prayer but is more personal and direct. We expand our petition to be delivered from sin to a plea that we also be delivered from the occasions that lead to sin.

From the Collect for Grace the service can move immediately into the offertory and the sermon. If the doxology is sung as an offertory response there may be no need for an additional hymn preceding the sermon.

Following the sermon a hymn may be sung. The worship concludes with the benediction: a final petition for the love of God in the person of the Trinity to grant peace and protection to the community of the faithful living in a world of aggressive evil.

While the writer does not suggest that this service be used in its entirety by The Methodist Church at large, he has been wooed by liturgical churches in the advantages of a standard procedure for Sunday morning worship.

Verney Johnstone (*Learning to Pray with the Church,* Longmans, Green & Co., o.p.), notes that, ". . . the great advantage of liturgy is that it does not depend on any particular minister or a particular set of worshippers. It is the voice of the Church and the voice of the Christian centuries, an accumulated treasury of devotion always ready for our jaded souls, always at the disposal of each successive generation."

The preceding appeared first in the May, 1955, issue of *The Pastor* by the author and is used here with the permission of the Editor.

MORNING PRAYER

Adapted from
THE SUNDAY SERVICE OF JOHN WESLEY

Let the service of worship begin at the time appointed. Let the people kneel or bow in silent prayer upon entering the church.

PRELUDE *The people in devout meditation.*

SENTENCES *One or more of them to be read by the minister, the people standing.*

The Lord is in his holy temple: let all the earth keep silence before him.

Let the words of my mouth, and the meditation of my heart, be acceptable in thy sight, O Lord, my strength, and my redeemer.

This is the day which the Lord hath made, we will rejoice and be glad in it.

The hour cometh, and now is, when the true worshipers shall worship the Father in spirit and in truth.

Advent. **Repent ye; for the kingdom of heaven is at hand. Prepare ye the way of the Lord, make straight in the desert a highway for our God.**

Christmas. **Behold, I bring you good tidings of great joy, which shall be to all people. For unto you is born this day in the city of David a Saviour, which is Christ the Lord.**

Epiphany. **From the rising of the sun even unto the going down of the same my name shall be great among the Gentiles; and in every place incense shall be offered unto my name, and a pure offering: for my name shall be great among the heathen, saith the Lord of hosts.**

Lent. **Rend your heart, and not your garments, and turn unto the Lord your God: for he is gracious and merciful, slow to anger, and of great kindness, and repenteth him of the evil.**

The sacrifices of God are a broken spirit: a broken and a contrite heart, O God, thou wilt not despise.

Good Friday. **Is it nothing to you, all ye that pass by? Behold, and see if there be any sorrow like unto my sorrow which is done unto me, wherewith the Lord hath afflicted me.**

In whom we have redemption through his blood, the forgiveness of sins, according to the riches of his grace.

Easter. **He is risen. The Lord is risen indeed. This is the day which the Lord hath made; we will rejoice and be glad in it.**

I will come to you. Because I live, ye shall live also.

Whitsunday. Ye shall receive power, after that the Holy Ghost is come upon you: and ye shall be witnesses unto me both in Jerusalem, and in all Judea, and in Samaria, and unto the uttermost part of the earth.

Trinity Sunday. Holy, holy, holy, Lord God Almighty, which was, and is, and is to come.

Thanksgiving Day. Honour the Lord with thy substance, and with the first fruits of all thine increase: so shall thy barns be filled with plenty, and thy presses shall burst out with new wine.

HYMN *If a processional, the hymn should precede the Sentences, and the people shall then rise and join in singing.*

CALL TO CONFESSION *By the minister, the people standing.*

Dearly beloved, the Scripture moveth us to acknowledge and confess our sins before Almighty God our heavenly Father with a humble, lowly, penitent, and obedient heart, to the end that we may obtain forgiveness by his infinite goodness and mercy. Wherefore I pray and beseech you, as many as are here present, to accompany me with a pure heart and a humble voice unto the throne of the heavenly grace. Let us pray.

GENERAL CONFESSION *To be said by all, the people seated and bowed or kneeling.*

Almighty and most merciful Father, we have erred and strayed from thy ways like lost sheep. We have followed too much the devices and desires of our own hearts. We have offended against thy holy laws. We have left undone those things which we ought to have done, and we have done those things which we ought not to have done. But thou, O Lord, have mercy upon us. Spare thou those, O God, who confess their faults. Restore thou those who are penitent, according to thy promises declared unto mankind in Christ Jesus our Lord. And grant, O most merciful Father, for his sake, that we may hereafter live a godly, righteous, and sober life; to the glory of thy holy name. *Amen.*

PRAYER FOR PARDON *The minister.*

O Lord, we beseech thee, absolve thy people from their offenses, that through thy bountiful goodness we may be delivered from the bonds of those sins which by our frailty we have committed. Grant this, O heavenly Father, for Jesus Christ's sake, our blessed Lord and Saviour. *Amen.*

The people shall answer here, and at the end of all other prayers, Amen.

THE LORD'S PRAYER *To be said by all.*

Our Father who art in heaven, hallowed be thy name; thy kingdom come thy will be done on earth as it is in heaven. Give us this day our daily bread. And forgive us our trespasses, as we forgive those who trespass against us. And lead us not into temptation, but deliver us from evil. For thine is the kingdom, and the power, and the glory, forever. *Amen.*

The Minister: O Lord, open Thou our lips.
***The People:* And our mouth shall show forth Thy praise.**
The Minister: Praise ye the Lord.
***The People:* The Lord's Name be praised.**

On Ash Wednesday and Good Friday the Venite may be omitted.

VENITE *To be said or sung by all, the people standing.*

O come, let us sing unto the Lord.
Let us heartily rejoice in the strength of our salvation.
Let us come before his presence with thanksgiving, and show ourselves glad in him with psalms.
For the Lord is a great God and a great King above all gods.
In his hand are all the corners of the earth: and the strength of the hills is his also.
The sea is his and he made it; and his hands prepared the dry land.
O come, let us worship and fall down, and kneel before the Lord our Maker.
For he is the Lord our God; and we are the people of his pastures, and the sheep of his hand.
O worship the Lord in the beauty of holiness; let the whole earth stand in awe of him.
For he cometh, for he cometh to judge the earth, and with righteousness to judge the world, and the people with his truth.

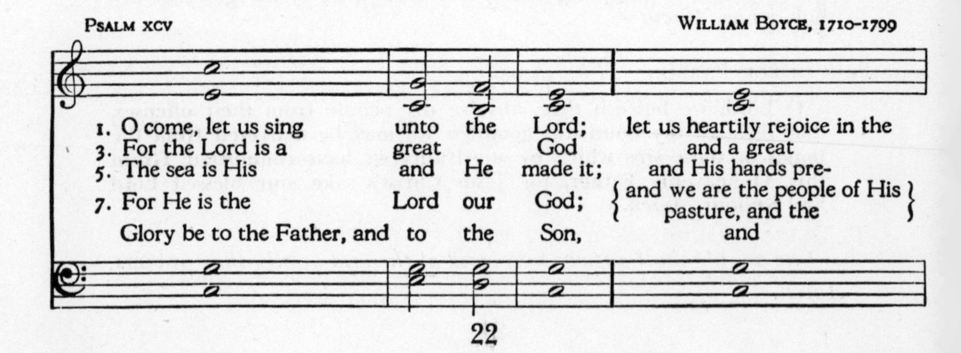

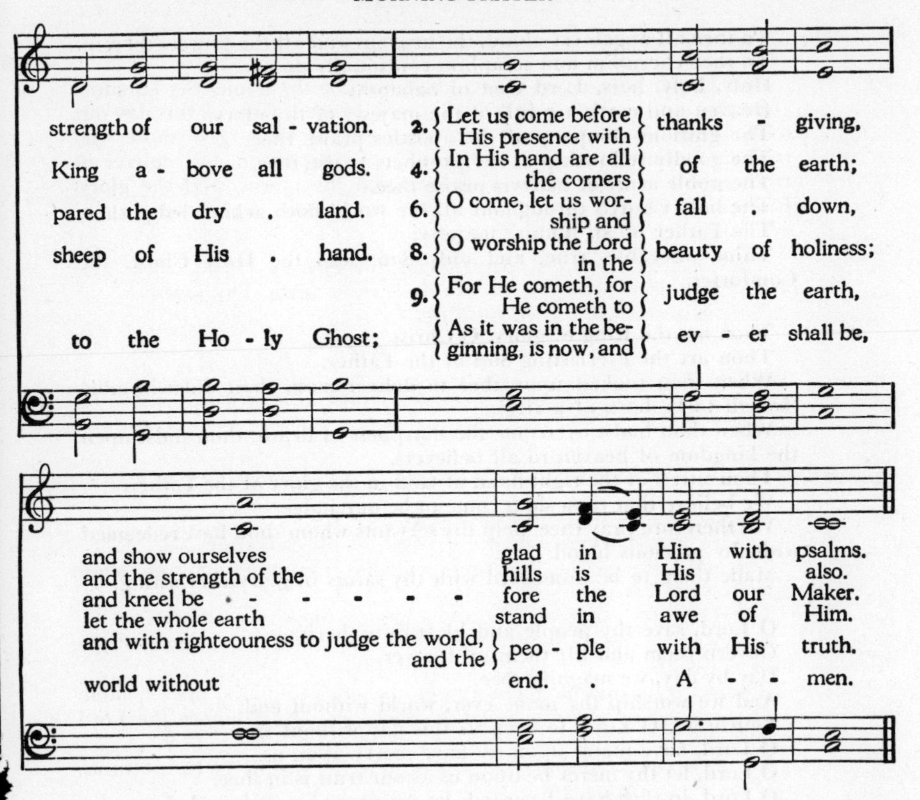
strength of our sal - vation. 2. { Let us come before His presence with } thanks - giving, and show ourselves glad in Him with psalms.
King a - bove all gods. 4. { In His hand are all the corners } of the earth; and the strength of the hills is His also.
pared the dry . land. 6. { O come, let us worship and } fall . down, and kneel be - fore the Lord our Maker.
sheep of His . hand. 8. { O worship the Lord in the } beauty of holiness; let the whole earth stand in awe of Him.
9. { For He cometh, for He cometh to } judge the earth, and with righteouness to judge the world, and the { peo - ple with His truth.
to the Ho - ly Ghost; { As it was in the beginning, is now, and } ev - er shall be, world without end. . A - - men.

PSALTER *To be said by all, the people standing.*

GLORIA PATRI *To be sung by all, the people standing.*

Glory be to the Father, and to the Son, and to the Holy Ghost; As it was in the beginning, is now, and ever shall be, world without end. *Amen.*

THE FIRST LESSON *The first lesson shall be a portion of the Old Testament, except when Holy Communion shall follow the reading of Morning Prayer, then the first lesson shall be a portion of the Epistle. The minister shall conclude the reading by saying, Here endeth the first lesson.*

TE DEUM *To be said or sung by all, the people standing.*

We praise thee, O God; we acknowledge thee to be the Lord.
All the earth doth worship thee, the Father everlasting.

To thee all angels cry aloud, the heavens and all the powers therein.
To thee cherubim and seraphim continually do cry,
Holy, holy, holy, Lord God of Sabaoth;
Heaven and earth are full of the majesty of thy glory.
The glorious company of the apostles praise thee.
The goodly fellowship of the prophets praise thee.
The noble army of martyrs praise thee.
The holy Church throughout all the world doth acknowledge thee;
The Father of an infinite majesty;
Thine adorable, true, and only Son; also the Holy Ghost, the Comforter.

Thou art the King of glory, O Christ.
Thou art the everlasting Son of the Father.
When thou tookest upon thee to deliver man, thou didst humble thy self to be born of a virgin.
When thou hadst overcome the sharpness of death, thou didst open the kingdom of heaven to all believers.
Thou sittest at the right hand of God in the glory of the Father.
We believe that thou shalt come to be our judge.
We therefore pray thee, help thy servants whom thou hast redeemed with thy precious blood.
Made them to be numbered with thy saints in glory everlasting.

O Lord, save thy people and bless thine heritage.
Govern them and lift them up forever.
Day by day, we magnify thee.
And we worship thy name ever, world without end.
Vouchsafe, O Lord, to keep us this day without sin.
O Lord, have mercy upon us, have mercy upon us.
O Lord, let thy mercy be upon us as our trust is in thee.
O Lord, in thee have I trusted; let me never be confounded.

HENRY LAWES, 1595–1662

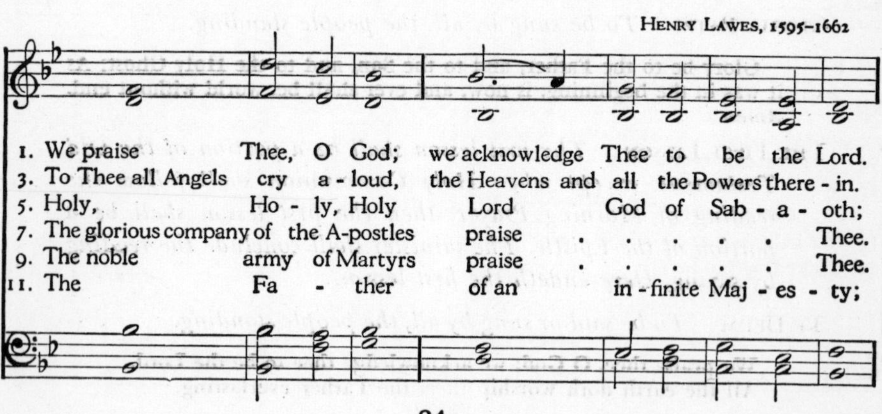
1. We praise Thee, O God; we acknowledge Thee to be the Lord.
3. To Thee all Angels cry a - loud, the Heavens and all the Powers there - in.
5. Holy, Ho - ly, Holy Lord God of Sab - a - oth;
7. The glorious company of the A-postles praise . . . . Thee.
9. The noble army of Martyrs praise . . . . Thee.
11. The Fa - ther of an in - finite Maj - es - ty;

2. All the earth doth worship Thee, the Father everlasting.
4. To Thee Cherubim and Ser-a-phim con-tin-ual-ly do cry,
6. Heaven and earth are full of the Maj-es-ty of Thy Glo-ry.
8. The goodly fellowship of the Prophets praise . . . . Thee.
10. The holy Church throughout all the world doth ac-knowl-edge Thee.
12. Thine a - - - - dor-able, true, and on - - ly Son;
13. Also the Ho-ly Ghost, the Com-fort-er.
ROBERT COOKE, 1768-1814
14. Thou art the King of Glory, O . . . . . Christ.
16. When Thou tookest upon Thee to de- liv-er man, Thou didst hum-ble Thyself to be born of a Virgin.
18. Thou sittest at the right hand of God in the Glo-ry of the Father.
20. We therefore pray Thee, help Thy servants whom Thou hast redeemed with Thy pre-cious blood.
15. Thou art the ever-last-ing Son of the Fa-ther.
17. When Thou hadst overcome the sharpness of death, Thou didst open the Kingdom of Heaven to all be-lievers.
19. We believe that Thou shalt come to be . our Judge.
21. Make them to be numbered with Thy Saints in glo-ry ev-er-lasting.

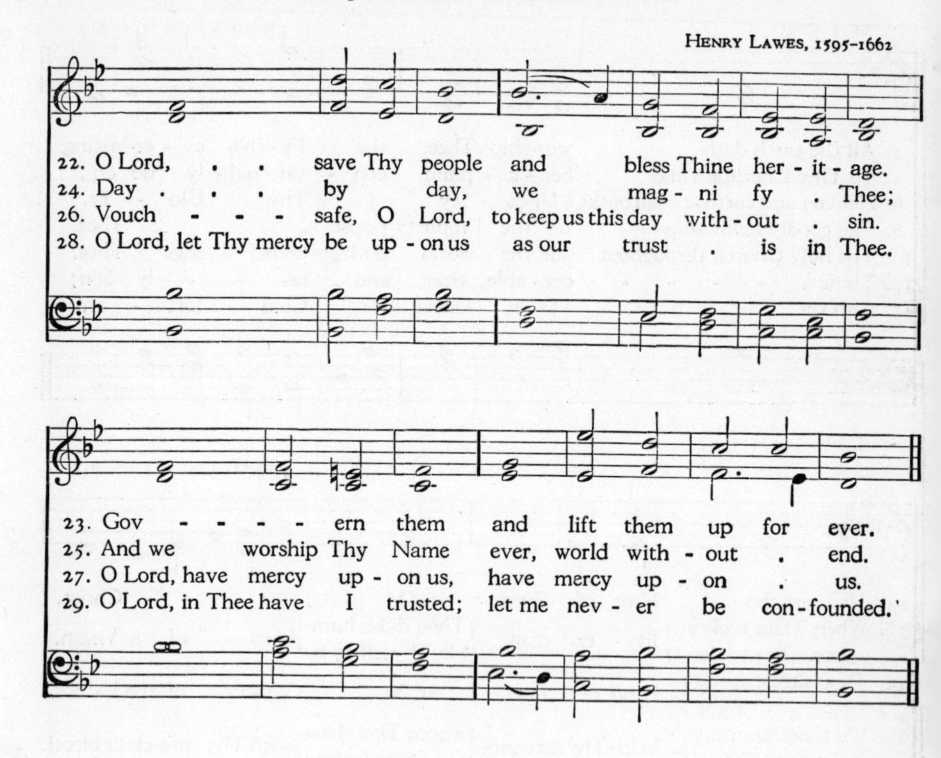

HENRY LAWES, 1595-1662
22. O Lord, . . save Thy people and bless Thine her - it - age.
24. Day . . . by day, we mag - ni fy . Thee;
26. Vouch - - - safe, O Lord, to keep us this day with - out . sin.
28. O Lord, let Thy mercy be up - on us as our trust . is in Thee.
23. Gov - - - - ern them and lift them up for ever.
25. And we worship Thy Name ever, world with - out . end.
27. O Lord, have mercy up - on us, have mercy up - on . us.
29. O Lord, in Thee have I trusted; let me nev - er be con - founded.

(Or this Canticle)

MAGNIFICAT *To be said or sung by all, the people standing, in place of the Te Deum.*

My soul doth magnify the Lord, and my spirit hath rejoiced in God my Savior.

For he hath regarded the lowliness of his handmaiden.

For behold, from henceforth all generations shall call me blessed.

For he that is mighty hath magnified me, and Holy is his name.

And his mercy is on them that fear him throughout all generations.

He hath showed strength with his arm; he hath scattered the proud in the imagination of their hearts.

He hath filled the hungry with good things, and the rich he hath sent empty away.

He, remembering his mercy hath holpen his servant Israel,

As he promised to our forefathers, Abraham and his seed, forever.

LUKE I. 46-55 HENRY SMART, 1813-1879

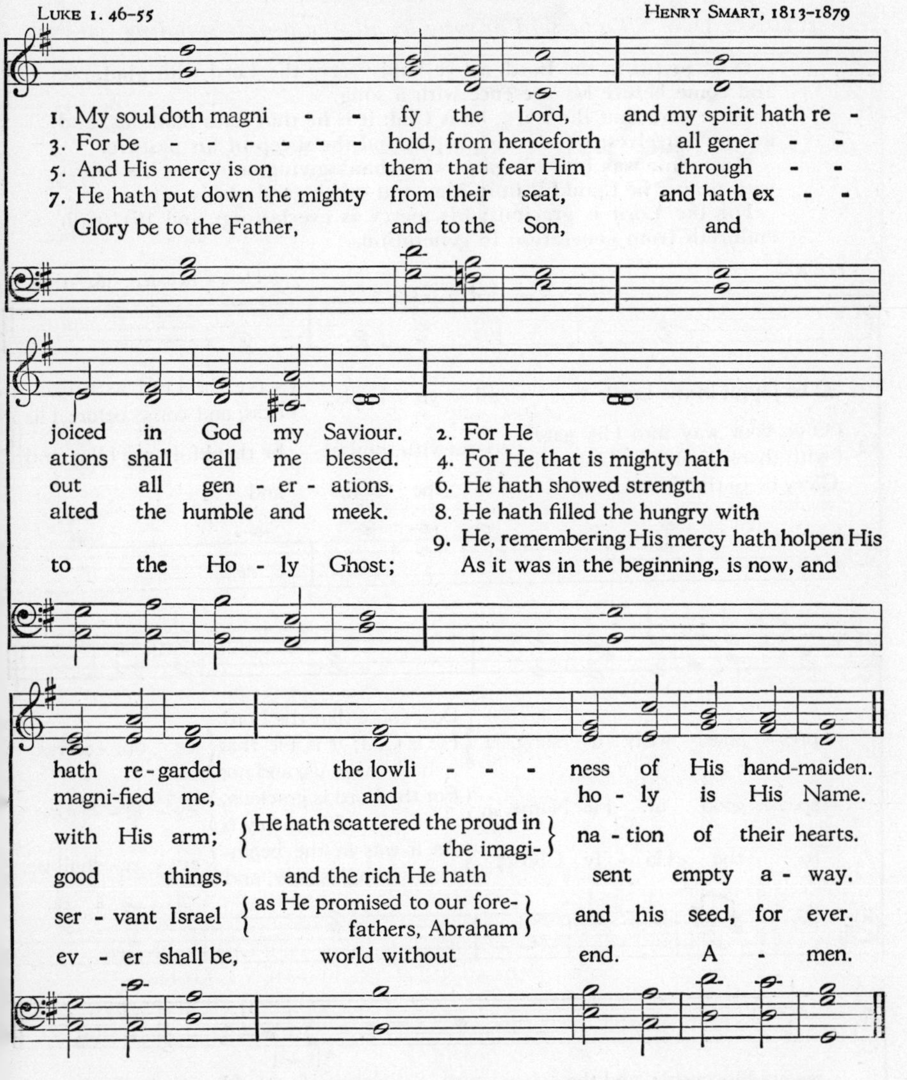

1. My soul doth magni - - fy the Lord, and my spirit hath re - joiced in God my Saviour.
3. For be - - - - - - - hold, from henceforth all gener - - ations shall call me blessed.
5. And His mercy is on them that fear Him through - - out all gen - er - ations.
7. He hath put down the mighty from their seat, and hath ex - - alted the humble and meek.
Glory be to the Father, and to the Son, and to the Ho - ly Ghost;
2. For He hath re-garded the lowli - - - ness of His hand-maiden.
4. For He that is mighty hath magni-fied me, and ho - ly is His Name.
6. He hath showed strength with His arm; He hath scattered the proud in the imagi- na - tion of their hearts.
8. He hath filled the hungry with good things, and the rich He hath sent empty a - way.
9. He, remembering His mercy hath holpen His ser - vant Israel as He promised to our fore-fathers, Abraham and his seed, for ever.
As it was in the beginning, is now, and ev - er shall be, world without end. A - men.

THE SECOND LESSON *The second lesson shall be a portion of the New Testament, except when Holy Communion shall follow the reading of Morning Prayer, then it shall be confined to the Gospel section only. The minister shall conclude the reading by saying, Here endeth the second lesson.*

JUBILATE DEO *To be said or sung by all, the people standing.*

O be joyful in the Lord, all ye lands; serve the Lord with gladness, and come before his presence with a song.

Be ye sure that the Lord, he is God; it is he that hath made us, and not we ourselves; we are his people, and the sheep of his pasture.

O go your way into his gates with thanksgiving, and into his courts with praise; be thankful unto him, and speak good of his name.

For the Lord is gracious; his mercy is everlasting; and his truth endureth from generation to generation.

PSALM C HENRY ALDRICH, 1647-1710

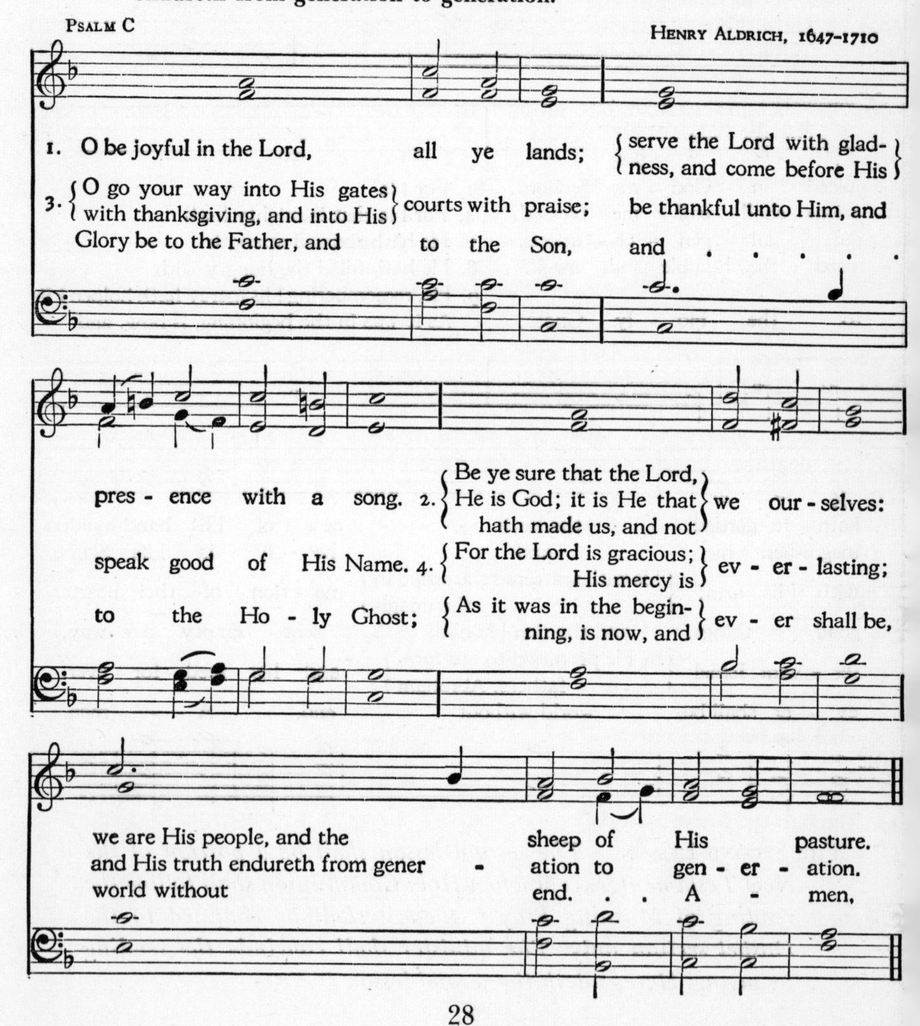

(Or this Canticle)

BENEDICTUS *To be said or sung by all, the people standing, in place of the Jubilate Deo.*

Blessed be the Lord God of Israel; for he hath visited and redeemed his people,

And hath raised up a mighty salvation for us in the house of his servant David;

As he spake by the mouth of his holy prophets, which have been since the world began:

That we should be saved from our enemies, and from the hand of all that hate us;

To perform the mercy promised to our forefathers, and to remember his holy covenant;

To perform the oath which he sware to our forefather Abraham, that he would give us;

That we, being delivered out of the hand of our enemies might serve him without fear,

In holiness and righteousness before him, all the days of our life.

And thou, child, shalt be called the prophet of the Highest, for thou shalt go before the face of the Lord, to prepare his ways;

To give knowledge of salvation unto his people for the remission of their sins,

Through the tender mercy of our God, whereby the dayspring from on high hath visited us,

To give light to them that sit in darkness, and in the shadow of death, and to guide our feet into the way of peace.

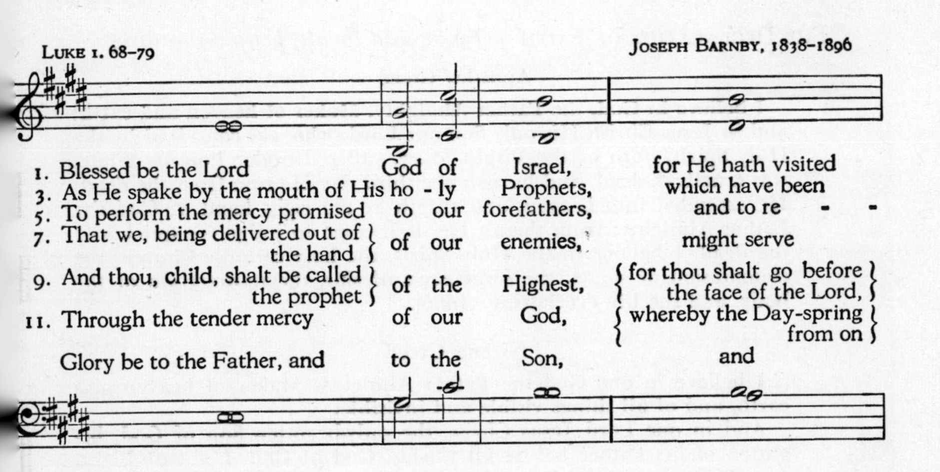
LUKE I. 68–79
JOSEPH BARNBY, 1838–1896
1. Blessed be the Lord God of Israel, for He hath visited
3. As He spake by the mouth of His ho - ly Prophets, which have been
5. To perform the mercy promised to our forefathers, and to re - -
7. That we, being delivered out of the hand of our enemies, might serve
9. And thou, child, shalt be called the prophet of the Highest, for thou shalt go before the face of the Lord,
11. Through the tender mercy of our God, whereby the Day-spring from on
Glory be to the Father, and to the Son, and

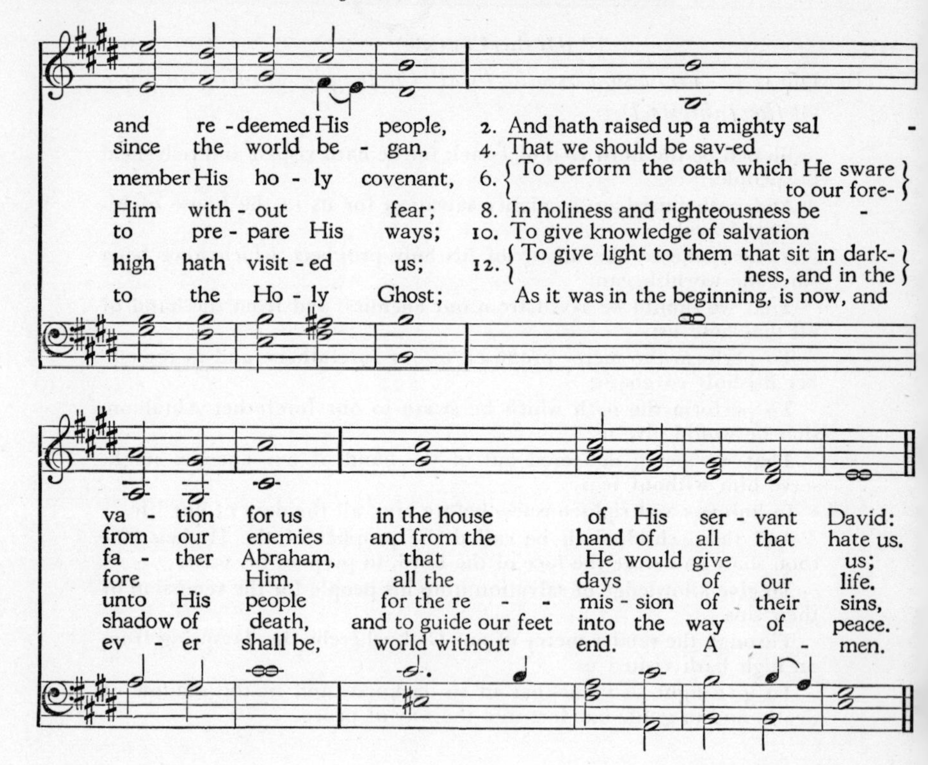
and re - deemed His people, 2. And hath raised up a mighty sal -
since the world be - gan, 4. That we should be sav-ed
member His ho - ly covenant, 6. { To perform the oath which He sware to our fore- }
Him with - out fear; 8. In holiness and righteousness be -
to pre - pare His ways; 10. To give knowledge of salvation
high hath visit - ed us; 12. { To give light to them that sit in dark- ness, and in the }
to the Ho - ly Ghost; As it was in the beginning, is now, and
va - tion for us in the house of His ser - vant David:
from our enemies and from the hand of all that hate us.
fa - ther Abraham, that He would give us;
fore Him, all the days of our life.
unto His people for the re - - mis - sion of their sins,
shadow of death, and to guide our feet into the way of peace.
ev - er shall be, world without end. A - - men.

THE DECLARATION OF FAITH *To be said by all, people standing.*

Apostles' Creed

I believe in God, the Father Almighty, Maker of heaven and earth; and in Jesus Christ, His only Son our Lord; who was conceived by the Holy Spirit, born of the Virgin Mary, suffered under Pontius Pilate, was crucified, dead, and buried; the third day He rose from the dead; He ascended into heaven, and sitteth at the right hand of God the Father Almighty; from thence He shall come to judge the quick and the dead. I believe in the Holy Spirit, the holy catholic Church, the communion of saints, the forgiveness of sins, the resurrection of the body, and the life everlasting. *Amen.*

Nicene Creed

I believe in one God the Father Almighty, Maker of heaven and earth, and of all things visible and invisible:

And in one Lord Jesus Christ, the only-begotten Son of God, begotten of his Father before all worlds, God of God, Light of Light, very God of very God, begotten not made, being of one substance

with the Father, by whom all things were made; who for us men and for our salvation came down from heaven, and was incarnated by the Holy Spirit of the Virgin Mary, and was made man, and was crucified also for us under Pontius Pilate; he suffered and was buried, and the third day he rose again according to the Scriptures, and ascended into heaven, and sitteth on the right hand of the Father; and he shall come again with glory, to judge both the quick and the dead, whose kingdom shall have no end.

And I believe in the Holy Spirit, the Lord and Giver of life, who proceedeth from the Father and the Son, who with the Father and the Son together is worshiped and glorified, who spake by the prophets. And I believe one catholic and apostolic Church. I acknowledge one baptism for the remission of sins. And I look for the resurrection of the dead, and the life of the world to come. *Amen.*

The Minister: The Lord be with you.
The People: **And with thy spirit.**
The Minister: Let us pray.

COLLECT FOR GRACE *To be said by all, the people seated and bowed, or kneeling.*

O Lord, our heavenly Father, almighty and everlasting God, who hast safely brought us to the beginning of this day; defend us in the same with thy mighty power; and grant that this day we fall into no sin, neither run into any kind of danger, but that all our doings may be ordered by thy governance, to do always that which is righteous in thy sight: through Jesus Christ our Lord. *Amen.*

PRAYER *Then may the minister offer a prayer, ending with: The grace of our Lord Jesus Christ, and the love of God, and the communion of the Holy Spirit, be with us all. Amen.*

OFFERTORY *Then may be sung an anthem, and an offering may be received.*

THE SERMON *Then the service is followed by a sermon or the Holy Communion, the minister shall make use of appropriate hymns and prayers. If the service is used for public or private use without sermon or Holy Communion then it may close with a hymn and the following benediction.*

BENEDICTION

The peace of God, which passeth all understanding, keep your hearts and minds in the knowledge and love of God, and of his Son Jesus Christ our Lord; and the blessing of God Almighty, the Father, the Son, and the Holy Spirit, be among you, and remain with you always. *Amen.*

EVENING PRAYER

EVENING PRAYER

To the receptive worshiper Evening Prayer can be a unique expression of his natural mood at the end of day. It is different from Morning Prayer in that there is less praise and more penitence. This is as it should be since at the end of day we are more reflective than at the beginning. In the sobering stillness of reflection we see a lengthy list of the times during the day when, "we have left undone those things which we ought to have done, and we have done those things which we ought not to have done."

Evening Prayer sets the stage for repentance. The call to confession and prayer of confession may well have a greater meaning now than it did when said so soon after awaking from a refreshing sleep. The Venite, described earlier as a hymn of praise, is deleted for Evening Prayer since it would be out of context with the general structure of the service. The Gloria in Excelsis, a Greek hymn known as the major doxology, may be sung at the end of the Psalm in place of the Gloria Patri. This may be done because of its stress on confession and forgiveness in the concluding stanzas.

One of the more obvious differences between Morning and Evening Prayer to the layman is the use of different canticles after the lessons. In Evening Prayer the Magnificat is sung after the first lesson. This canticle has been found in the liturgical offices since the fourth century. It is Mary's song of greeting at the meeting of the mother of John the Baptist in Luke 1:46-54. The writer of the Magnificat must have modeled his song after the Song of Hannah in I Samuel 2:1-10. The theme of both is hope for the lowly, meek, hungry, and poor. This theme supports the mood of Evening Prayer. Like the Benedictus, the Magnificat is the perfect link between the Old and New Testament lessons. The canticle recalls the promises of God to Abraham and the continuing promises of help to Israel to be given in the form of a Saviour.

Occasionally the Bonum est may be sung in place of the Magnificat. This canticle from Psalm 92 was first used in the Temple at the morning sacrifice on the Sabbath. Its usage at this juncture is peculiar to American Prayer Books only.

The second lesson concludes with the Song of Simeon called the Nunc dimittis from Luke 2:29. Like the Magnificat its usage dates back to the fourth century. While the Song of Mary anticipates the birth of Jesus, this canticle, coming after the reading of the New Testament, looks now upon it as an accomplished fact. The last stanza of the Nunc dimittis gives a universal touch to the gospel and leads quite naturally into the affirmation of faith.

The rehearsing of the creed and those devotional exercises following are similar to the concluding phrases of Morning Prayer. Evening Prayer might well end with the bidding prayers called collects. Some services might even end with sentence prayers from the congregation. Since the mood of Evening Prayer is intimately penitential any personal touch that would augment this mood without being offensive to the orderliness of the service should not be overlooked.

EVENING PRAYER

Adapted from

THE SUNDAY SERVICE OF

JOHN WESLEY AND THE BOOK OF COMMON PRAYER

Let the people kneel or bow in silent prayer upon entering the church.

PRELUDE *The people in devout meditation.*

SENTENCES *One or more of them to be read by the minister, the people standing.*

The Lord is in his holy temple: let all the earth keep silence before him.

Lord, I have loved the habitation of thy house, the place where thine honour dwelleth.

Let my prayer be set forth in thy sight as the incense; and let the lifting up of my hands be an evening sacrifice.

Advent. **Watch ye, for ye know not when the master of the house cometh, at even, or at midnight, or at the cock-crowing, or in the morning; lest coming suddenly he find you sleeping.**

Christmas. **Behold, the tabernacle of God is with men, and he will dwell with them, and they shall be his people, and God himself shall be with them, and be their God.**

Epiphany. **The Gentiles shall come to thy light, and kings to the brightness of thy rising.**

We have also a more sure word of prophecy; whereunto ye do well that ye take heed, as unto a light that shineth in a dark place, until the day dawn, and the day star arise in your hearts.

Lent. **Come ye, and let us walk in the light of the Lord, He will teach us of his ways, and we will walk in his paths.**

In returning and rest shall ye be saved; in quietness and in confidence shall be your strength.

If we say that we have no sin, we deceive ourselves, and the truth is not in us; but if we confess our sins, God is faithful and just to forgive us our sins, and to cleanse us from all unrighteousness.

Good Friday. **All we like sheep have gone astray; we have turned every one to his own way; and the Lord hath laid on him the iniquity of us all.**

Easter. **Thanks be to God, which giveth us the victory through our Lord Jesus Christ.**

If ye then be risen with Christ, seek those things which are above, where Christ sitteth on the right hand of God.

Whitsunday. **It shall come to pass, that I will pour out my spirit upon all flesh; and your sons and your daughters shall prophesy, your old men shall dream dreams, your**

young men shall see visions: and also upon the servants and upon the handmaids will I pour out my spirit.

Trinity Sunday. Holy, holy, holy, is the Lord of hosts: the whole earth is full of his glory.

Kingdomtide. They that be wise shall shine as the brightness of the firmament; and they that turn many to righteousness as the stars for ever and ever.

Thou crownest the year with thy goodness. The pastures are clothed with flocks; the valleys also are covered over with corn; they shout for joy, they also sing.

HYMN *If a processional, the hymn should precede the Sentences, and the people shall then rise and join in singing.*

CALL TO CONFESSION *By the minister, the people standing.*

Dearly beloved, the Scripture moveth us to acknowledge and confess our sins before Almighty God our heavenly Father with a humble, lowly, penitent, and obedient heart, to the end that we may obtain forgiveness by his infinite goodness and mercy. Wherefore I pray and beseech you, as many as are here present, to accompany me with a pure heart and a humble voice unto the throne of the heavenly grace. Let us pray.

GENERAL CONFESSION *To be said by all, the people seated and bowed or kneeling.*

Almighty and most merciful Father, we have erred and strayed from thy ways like lost sheep. We have followed too much the devices and desires of our own hearts. We have offended against thy holy laws. We have left undone those things which we ought to have done, and we have done those things which we ought not to have done. But thou, O Lord, have mercy upon us. Spare thou those, O God, who confess their faults. Restore thou those who are penitent, according to thy promises declared unto mankind in Christ Jesus our Lord. And grant, O most merciful Father, for his sake, that we may hereafter live a godly, righteous, and sober life; to the glory of thy holy name. *Amen.*

PRAYER FOR PARDON *The minister.*

O Lord, we beseech thee, absolve thy people from their offenses, that through thy bountiful goodness we may be delivered from the bonds of those sins which by our frailty we have committed. Grant this, O heavenly Father, for Jesus Christ's sake, our blessed Lord and Saviour. *Amen.*

The people shall answer here, and at the end of all other prayers, AMEN.

THE LORD'S PRAYER *To be said by all.*

Our Father who art in heaven, hallowed be thy name; thy kingdom come; thy will be done on earth as it is in heaven. Give us this day our daily bread. And forgive us our trespasses, as we forgive those who trespass against us. And lead us not into temptation, but deliver us from evil. For thine is the kingdom, and the power, and the glory, forever. ***Amen.***

The Minister: O Lord, open Thou our lips.
The People: **And our mouth shall show forth Thy praise.**
The Minister: Praise ye the Lord.
The People: **The Lord's Name be praised.**

PSALTER *To be said by all, the people standing. Following the Psalter may be sung the Gloria Patri or Gloria in Excelsis.*

GLORIA PATRI

Glory be to the Father, and to the Son, and to the Holy Ghost; As it was in the beginning, is now, and ever shall be, world without end. ***Amen.***

or

GLORIA IN EXCELSIS

Glory be to God on high.
And on earth peace, good will toward men.
We praise thee, we bless thee, we worship thee, we glorify thee.
We give thanks to thee for thy great glory, O Lord God, heavenly King, God the Father Almighty!
O Lord, the only-begotten Son Jesus Christ; O Lord God, Lamb of God, Son of the Father, that takest away the sins of the world, have mercy upon us.
Thou that takest away the sins of the world, receive our prayer.
Thou that sittest at the right hand of God the Father, have mercy upon us.
For thou only art holy; thou only art the Lord.
Thou only, O Christ, with the Holy Ghost, art most high in the glory of God the Father. ***Amen.***

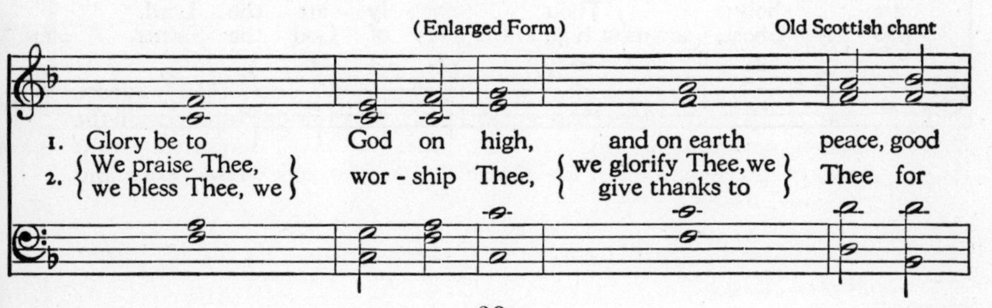
(Enlarged Form)
Old Scottish chant
1. Glory be to God on high, and on earth peace, good
2. We praise Thee, we bless Thee, we wor - ship Thee, we glorify Thee, we give thanks to Thee for

will toward men. 3. O Lord God, Heaven - ly King;
Thy great glory. 4. O Lord, the only-begotten Son, Je - sus Christ,
Slowly
God, the Fa - ther Al - mighty. 5. That takest away the
O Lord God, Lamb of God, Son . . of the Father, 6. Thou that takest away the
7. Thou that takest away the
8. Thou that sittest at the right hand of
sins of the world, have mercy up - on us. 9. For Thou only
sins of the world, have mercy up - on us. 10. Thou only, O Christ, with the
sins of the world, re - ceive our prayer.
God the Fa - ther, have mercy up - on us.
art . . holy; Thou on - ly art the Lord.
Ho - ly Ghost, art most high in the glory of God the Father. A - MEN.

THE FIRST LESSON *The first lesson shall be a portion of the Old Testament, except when Holy Communion shall follow the reading of Evening Prayer, then the first lesson shall be a portion of the Epistle. The minister shall conclude the reading by saying, Here endeth the first lesson.*

MAGNIFICAT *To be said or sung by all, the people standing.*

My soul doth magnify the Lord, and my spirit hath rejoiced in God my Saviour.

For he hath regarded the lowliness of his handmaiden.

For behold, from henceforth all generations shall call me blessed.

For he that is mighty hath magnified me, and Holy is his Name.

And his mercy is on them that fear him throughout all generations.

He hath showed strength with his arm; he hath scattered the proud in the imagination of their hearts.

He hath filled the hungry with good things, and the rich he hath sent empty away.

He, remembering his mercy hath holpen his servant Israel,

As he promised to our forefathers, Abraham and his seed, forever.

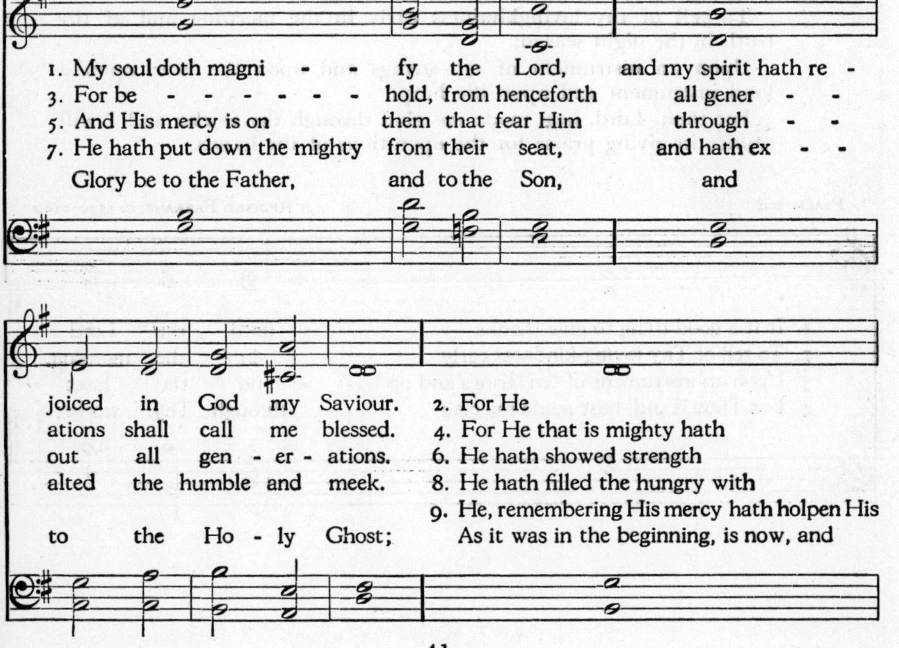

LUKE I. 46-55
HENRY SMART, 1813-1879
1. My soul doth magni - fy the Lord, and my spirit hath re - joiced in God my Saviour.
3. For be - - - - - - hold, from henceforth all gener - - ations shall call me blessed.
5. And His mercy is on them that fear Him through - - out all gen - er - ations.
7. He hath put down the mighty from their seat, and hath ex - - alted the humble and meek.
Glory be to the Father, and to the Son, and to the Ho - ly Ghost;
2. For He
4. For He that is mighty hath
6. He hath showed strength
8. He hath filled the hungry with
9. He, remembering His mercy hath holpen His
As it was in the beginning, is now, and

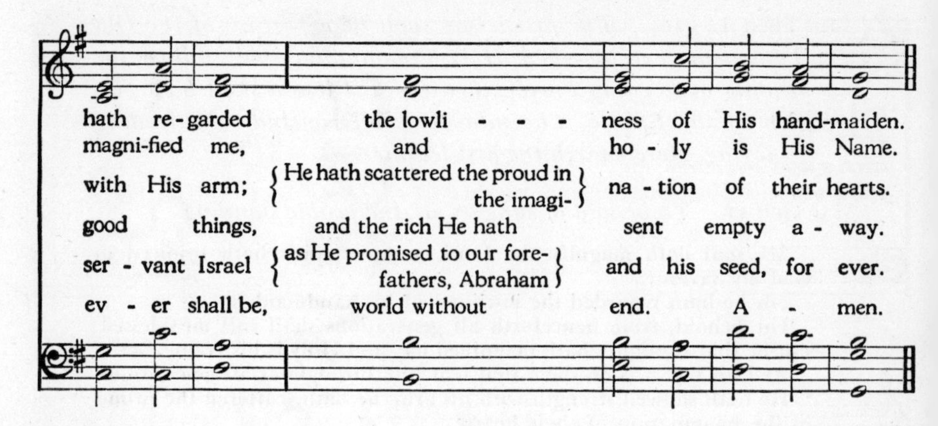
hath re-garded the lowli - - - ness of His hand-maiden.
magni-fied me, and ho - ly is His Name.
with His arm; He hath scattered the proud in the imagi- na - tion of their hearts.
good things, and the rich He hath sent empty a - way.
ser - vant Israel as He promised to our fore-fathers, Abraham and his seed, for ever.
ev - er shall be, world without end. A - men.

(Or this Canticle)

BONUM EST

It is a good thing to give thanks unto the Lord, and to sing praises unto thy name, O most Highest;

To tell of thy lovingkindness early in the morning and of thy truth in the night season;

Upon an instrument of ten strings and upon the lute; upon a loud instrument and upon the harp.

For thou, Lord, hast made me glad through thy works; and I will rejoice in giving praise for the operations of thy hands.

PSALM XCII — RICHARD FARRANT, c. 1530–1580

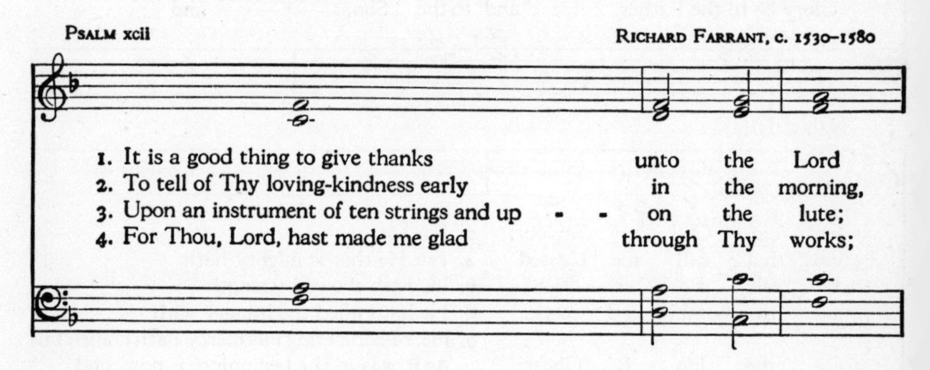
1. It is a good thing to give thanks unto the Lord
2. To tell of Thy loving-kindness early in the morning,
3. Upon an instrument of ten strings and up - - on the lute;
4. For Thou, Lord, hast made me glad through Thy works;

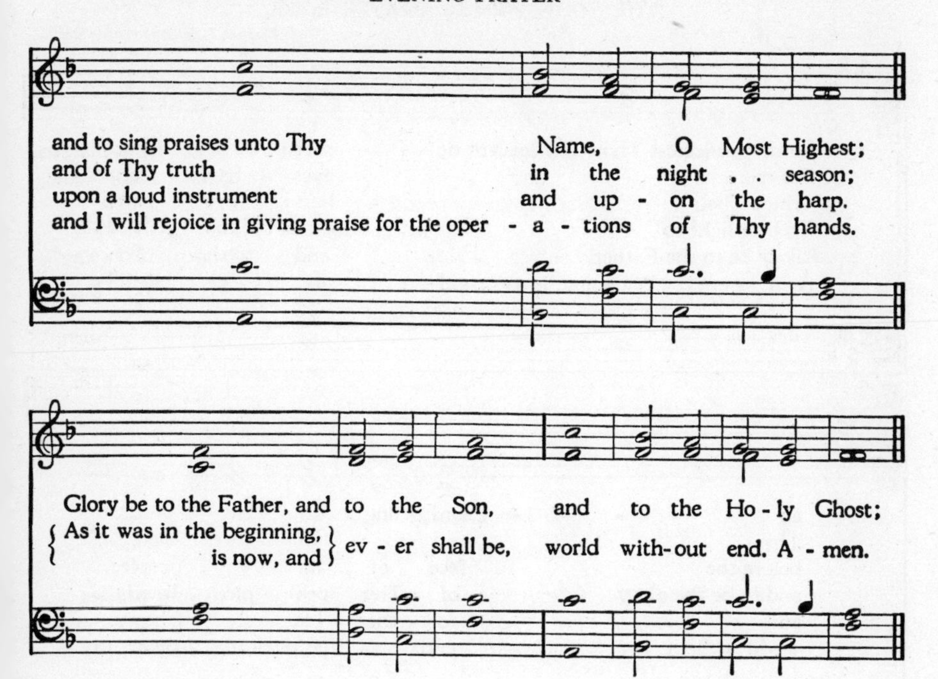
and to sing praises unto Thy Name, O Most Highest;
and of Thy truth in the night . . season;
upon a loud instrument and up - on the harp.
and I will rejoice in giving praise for the oper - a - tions of Thy hands.
Glory be to the Father, and to the Son, and to the Ho - ly Ghost;
As it was in the beginning, is now, and ev - er shall be, world with-out end. A - men.

THE SECOND LESSON *The second lesson shall be a portion of the New Testament, except when Holy Communion shall follow the reading of Evening Prayer, then it shall be confined to the Gospel section only. The minister shall conclude the reading by saying, Here endeth the second lesson.*

NUNC DIMITTIS *To be said or sung by all, people standing.*

Lord, now lettest thou thy servant depart in peace, according to thy words,

For mine eyes have seen thy salvation,

Which thou hast prepared before the face of all people;

To be a light to lighten the Gentiles and to be the glory of the people, Israel.

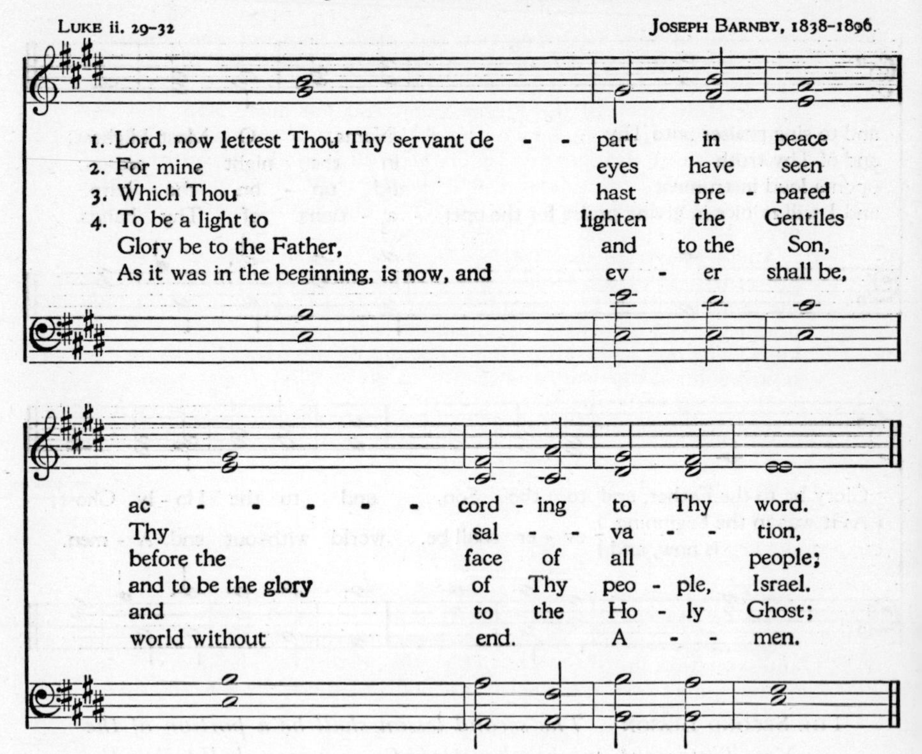
LUKE ii. 29-32
JOSEPH BARNBY, 1838-1896
1. Lord, now lettest Thou Thy servant de - - part in peace
2. For mine eyes have seen
3. Which Thou hast pre - pared
4. To be a light to lighten the Gentiles
Glory be to the Father, and to the Son,
As it was in the beginning, is now, and ev - er shall be,
ac - - - - - cord - ing to Thy word.
Thy sal - - va - - tion,
before the face of all people;
and to be the glory of Thy peo - ple, Israel.
and to the Ho - ly Ghost;
world without end. A - - men.

AFFIRMATION OF FAITH *To be said by all, people standing.*

Apostles' Creed

I believe in God, the Father Almighty, Maker of heaven and earth; and in Jesus Christ, His only Son our Lord; who was conceived by the Holy Spirit, born of the Virgin Mary, suffered under Pontius Pilate, was crucified, dead, and buried; the third day He rose from the dead; He ascended into heaven, and sitteth at the right hand of God the Father Almighty; from thence He shall come to judge the quick and the dead. I believe in the Holy Spirit, the holy catholic Church, the communion of saints, the forgiveness of sins, the resurrection of the body, and the life everlasting. ***Amen.***

Nicene Creed

I believe in one God the Father Almighty, Maker of heaven and earth, and of all things visible and invisible:

And in one Lord Jesus Christ, the only-begotten Son of God, begotten of his Father before all worlds, God of God, Light of Light,

very God of very God, begotten not made, being of one substance with the Father, by whom all things were made; who for us men and for our salvation came down from heaven, and was incarnated by the Holy Spirit of the Virgin Mary, and was made man, and was crucified also for us under Pontius Pilate; he suffered and was buried, and the third day he rose again according to the Scriptures, and ascended into heaven, and sitteth on the right hand of the Father; and he shall come again with glory, to judge both the quick and the dead, whose kingdom shall have no end.

And I believe in the Holy Spirit, the Lord and Giver of life, who proceedeth from the Father and the Son, who with the Father and the Son together is worshiped and glorified, who spake by the prophets. And I believe one catholic and apostolic Church. I acknowledge one baptism for the remission of sins. And I look for the resurrection of the dead, and the life of the world to come. *Amen.*

The Minister: The Lord be with you.
The People: And with thy spirit.
The Minister: Let us pray.

A COLLECT FOR PEACE *Minister and people.*

O God, from whom all holy desires, all good counsels, and all just works do proceed; give unto thy servants that peace which the world cannot give; that our hearts may be set to obey thy commandments, and also that by thee, we, being defended from the fear of our enemies, may pass our time in rest and quietness; through the merits of Jesus Christ our Saviour. *Amen.*

(Or this Collect)

O God, the Creator and Preserver of all mankind, we humbly beseech thee for all sorts and conditions of men; that thou wouldest be pleased to make thy ways known unto them, thy saving health unto all nations. More especially we pray for thy holy Church universal; that it may be so guided and governed by thy good Spirit, that all who profess and call themselves Christians may be led into the way of truth, and hold the faith in unity of spirit, in the bond of peace and in righteousness of life. Finally we commend to thy fatherly goodness all those who are in any way afflicted, or distressed, in mind, body, or estate; that it may please thee to comfort and relieve them, according o their several necessities; giving them patience under their sufferings, and a happy issue out of all their afflictions. And this we beg for Jesus Christ's sake. *Amen.*

(Or this Collect)

Lighten our darkness, we beseech thee, O Lord; and by thy great mercy defend us from all perils and dangers of this night; for the love of thy only Son, our Saviour, Jesus Christ. *Amen.*

(Or this Collect)

Direct us, O Lord, in all our doings, with thy most gracious favor, and further us with thy continual help, that in all our works, begun, continued, and ended in thee, we may glorify thy holy name, and finally, by thy mercy, obtain everlasting life; through Jesus Christ our Lord. *Amen.*

(Or this Collect)

Almighty God, who hast given us grace at this time with one accord to make our common supplications unto thee; and doest promise that when two or three are gathered together in thy Name thou wilt grant their requests; fulfil now, O Lord, the desires and petitions of thy servants, as may be most expedient for them; granting us in this world knowledge of thy truth, and the world to come life everlasting. *Amen.*

PRAYER *Then may the minister offer a prayer, ending with: The peace of our Lord Jesus Christ, and the love of God, and the communion of the Holy Spirit, be with us all.* AMEN.

OFFERTORY *Then may be sung an anthem, and an offering may be received.*

SERMON *When the service is followed by a sermon or the Holy Communion, the minister shall make use of appropriate hymns and prayers. If the service is used for public or private use without sermon or Holy Communion then it may close with a hymn and the following benediction.*

BENEDICTION

The peace of God, which passeth all understanding, keep your hearts and minds in the knowledge and love of God, and of his Son Jesus Christ our Lord; and the blessing of God Almighty, the Father, the Son, and the Holy Spirit, be among you, and remain with you always. *Amen.*

A GENERAL SUPPLICATION

A GENERAL SUPPLICATION

SUPPLICATION IS THE GREEK TRANSLATION FOR the word litany. The following service appears in the Book of Common Prayer under the heading, "The Litany."

The use of litanies in worship first began in the liturgically conscious fourth century. Monks in a monastery at Antioch developed a system of singing certain Psalms with brief responses after each verse. This pattern of antiphonal chanting was adopted by other Christian liturgists and applied to corporate prayers and other devotional acts.

Litanies were often sung in Christian processions to counteract pagan or heretical demonstrations. It was, therefore, natural that these musical supplications should in time be substituted for the ancient pagan rites surrounding spring planting, harvest, and the protecting of the stored grain from rot and mildew. Litanies were also written for special occasions. The first English litany was published in 1544 during Henry VIII's war with France.

Today the Litany is used as an occasional introduction to Holy Communion or Morning or Evening Prayer. The use of the Litany is especially appropriate during Lent because of its deep reflective and penitential mood and is often used in conjunction with the Penitential Office in the Book of Common Prayer.

In the following adaptation of the Litany there are three major parts. 1. The Invocation which is the calling upon God is His three manifestations to be merciful toward His children. 2. The Deprecation which is the calling upon the Lord to deliver us from all kinds of evil. The final deprecations have been changed from the way they appear in the Prayer Book, but for the most part the petitions are timeless and valid for every age and class of people. 3. The Sufferages expand our concern beyond the boundaries of our own needs. These petitions remind us that God is assiduous to every area of life and we would do well to mirror His concern. The sufferages end with a form of the Agnus Dei, which is usually incorporated in the Gloria in excelsis and the Lord's Prayer.

The Supplication ends with a succinct prayer of our complete dependance upon God, ". . . and for the glory of thy Name, turn from us all those evils that we most justly have deserved; and grant that in all our troubles we may put our whole trust and confidence in thy mercy, . . ." This concludes in a most fitting way our supplication for a renewed spiritual concern, not only a personal, but a universal concern.

A GENERAL SUPPLICATION

Adapted from

THE BOOK OF COMMON PRAYER

Let the people kneel or bow in silent prayer upon entering the church.

HYMN *If a processional the people shall rise and join in singing.*

INVOCATION *The people standing, minister leading, people responding.*

O God the Father, Creator of heaven and earth;
Have mercy upon us.
O God the Son, Redeemer of the world;
Have mercy upon us.
O God the Holy Ghost, Sanctifier of the faithful;
Have mercy upon us.
O holy, blessed and glorious Trinity, one God;
Have mercy upon us.

DEPRECATION *The people seated and bowed or kneeling, responding.*

Remember not, Lord, our offences, nor the offences of our forefathers; neither take thou vengeance of our sins; Spare us, good Lord, spare thy people, whom thou hast redeemed with thy most precious blood, and be not angry with us for ever.

Spare us, good Lord.

From all evil and mischief; from sin; from the crafts and assaults of the devil; from thy wrath, and from everlasting damnation,

Good Lord, deliver us.

From all blindness of heart; from pride, vainglory, and hypocrisy, from envy, hatred, and malice, and all uncharitableness,

Good Lord, deliver us.

From all inordinate and sinful affections, and from all the deceits of the world,

Good Lord, deliver us.

From war's bloody way and the aftermath of plague, pestilence, and famine,

Good Lord, deliver us.

From false love of country that blinds us to thy call; from hardness of heart; from contempt of thy holy Gospel,

Good Lord, deliver us.

THE SUFFRAGES *The people still in an attitude of prayer, responding.*

We sinners do beseech thee to hear us, O Lord God; and that it may please thee to rule and govern thy holy Church universal according to thy Holy Will.
We beseech thee to hear us, good Lord.
That it may please thee so to rule the heart of thy servant, The President of the United States, that he may above all things seek thy honour, glory, and love;
We beseech thee to hear us, good Lord.
That it may please thee to bless and direct all public officials, giving them grace to execute justice, and to maintain truth;
We beseech thee to hear us, good Lord.
That it may please thee to illuminate all thy ministers with true knowledge and understanding of thy Word, and that both by their preaching and living they may set forth, and show it accordingly;
We beseech thee to hear us, good Lord.
That it may please thee to send forth laborers into thy harvest;
We beseech thee to hear us, good Lord.
That it may please thee to give to all nations unity, peace, and concern;
We beseech thee to hear us, good Lord.
That it may please thee to give us an heart to love and fear thee, and diligently to live after thy commandments;
We beseech thee to hear us, good Lord.
That it may please thee to give to all thy people increase of grace to hear receptively thy Word, and to receive it with pure affection, and to bring forth the fruits of the Spirit;
We beseech thee to hear us, good Lord.
That it may please thee to bring into the way of truth all such as have erred, and have deceived;
We beseech thee to hear us, good Lord.
That it may please thee to strengthen such as do stand; and to comfort and help the weak-hearted; and to raise up those who fall; and finally to beat down Satan under our feet;
We beseech thee to hear us, good Lord.
That it may please thee to succour, help, and comfort, all who are in danger, necessity, and tribulation;
We beseech thee to hear us, good Lord.
That it may please thee to preserve all who travel by land, by water, or by air, all sick persons, and young children, and to show pity upon all prisoners and captives;
We beseech thee to hear us, good Lord.
That it may please thee to defend, and provide for, the fatherless children, and widows, and all who are desolate and oppressed;
We beseech thee to hear us, good Lord.
That it may please thee to have mercy upon all men;
We beseech thee to hear us, good Lord.

That it may please thee to forgive our enemies, persecutors, and slanderers, and to turn their hearts;
We beseech thee to hear us, good Lord.

That it may please thee to give us true repentance; to forgive us all our sins, negligences, and ignorances; and to endue us with the grace of thy Holy Spirit to amend our lives according to thy holy Word;
We beseech thee to hear us, good Lord.

AGNUS DEI *The people still in an attitude of prayer, responding.*

Son of God, we beseech thee to hear us.
Son of God, we beseech thee to hear us.
O Lamb of God, who takest away the sins of the world;
Grant us thy peace.
O Lamb of God, who takest away the sins of the world;
Have mercy upon us.
O Christ, hear us.
O Christ, hear us.
Lord, have mercy upon us.
Lord, have mercy upon us.
Christ, have mercy upon us.
Christ, have mercy upon us.
Lord, have mercy upon us.
Lord, have mercy upon us.

THE LORD'S PRAYER

Our Father, who art in heaven, hallowed be thy name; thy kingdom come; thy will be done on earth as it is in heaven. Give us this day our daily bread. And forgive us our trespasses, as we forgive those who trespass against us. And lead us not into temptation, but deliver us from evil. For thine is the kingdom, and the power, and the glory, forever. ***Amen.***

THE COLLECT *To be prayed by all.*

We humbly beseech thee, O Father, mercifully to look upon our infirmities; and for the glory of thy Name, turn from us all those evils that we most justly have deserved; and grant that in all our troubles we may put our whole trust and confidence in thy mercy, and evermore serve thee in holiness and pureness of living, to thy honour and glory; through our only Mediator and Advocate, Jesus Christ our Lord. ***Amen.***

The minister may end the Supplication here, or if Holy Communion is to follow begin with the Prayer of Consecration, if Morning or Evening Prayer is to follow begin with the versicle at the end of the Lord's Prayer.

A SERVICE OF PENITENCE

A SERVICE OF PENITENCE

PENITENTIAL OFFICES ARE CONSPICUOUSLY ABSENT FROM most Protestant prayer books. Certain radical reform groups made sure that those practices which the Catholic Church had sponsored and with doubtful Scriptural counterpart were deleted. Such indiscriminate pruning could not help but lose for the Protestant Church some vital worship experiences. Not the least of our losses was the penitential office.

Today theology and science are witnessing a change of thought about man. We are redefining man in terms of recent nuclear achievements. The predominate opinion seems to be that the flimsy material from which man has been constructing his religion will not stand the impact of atomic pressures. The sins of world tensions and explosions are upon us all and we need to be constantly aware of them. We need to say often, "Wash me thoroughly from my wickedness, and cleanse me from my sin." Thus, a penitential office is included in this book.

The service of penitence may be used as a private devotional exercise or as a public prefix to Holy Communion, Morning or Evening Prayer, and The Supplication. If used publicly one of these services should follow the service of penitence to better complete the worship experience.

The service begins with the responsive reading of Psalm 51. This Psalm has been ascribed to David and is thought to be his lament for his sin against Uriah. While our sins may not have been as great as that of David we still need to rehearse the words of repentance. Our murderings have been committed by words of gossip, cruel glances, and sinister thoughts.

The Psalmist, whether it was David or a much later poet, recognizes that in the final analysis all sin is committed against God and Him only. With this weight upon our minds we are driven to repent of all officiousness against man or God. In the concluding verses we pledge our renewed services to God and promise with His help to guide others back to Him. This dedication is essential if our penitence is to be real and lasting.

Since we have not the strength to pledge or promise ourselves to God we cry to the Lord for his merciful help in the Kyrie: "Lord, have mercy upon us." The Lord's Prayer gives added support to our plea for guidance and deliverance from sin and temptation. The Versicles that follow the Lord's Prayer are from Psalms 86, 20, 79, and continues the cry for help in our turning from sin to the service of the Lord.

The first collect is the Collect of the Penitential Office in *The Book of Common Prayer.* The second collect was composed by Cranmer from several sources. He used prayers from the blessing of the ashes and prayers from the Sarum. Certain phrases have been used in the "Prayer of Humble Access" in the Holy Communion. The prayer also contains certain phrases from the Psalms. The mood of repentance is continued in these collects.

The anthem, so named because it was sung antiphonally in the medieval office during the distribution of ashes on Ash Wednesday, is a hymn to the goodness and mercy of God. A God, who is "full of compassion, long-suffering and of great pity."

The congregation has now traveled from the depths of depression, when they voiced their sins before God; through the uplands of pledge and promise; to the final summit, when God's mercies were displayed before them. Now the penitent is assured that God does not want a single sinner to die without first being forgiven of his sins. Following the prayer for pardon the service may conclude with the benediction or it may lead into one of the previously mentioned services.

A SERVICE OF PENITENCE

Adapted from
THE BOOK OF COMMON PRAYER

This service may be used as a private devotional practice during Lent.

This service may also be used as a penitential introduction to Holy Communion, Morning or Evening Prayer, or the Supplication.

THE PSALM OF PENITENCE *To be said responsively when used as public worship.*

Have mercy upon me, O God, after thy great goodness; according to the multitude of thy mercies do away mine offenses.

Wash me thoroughly from my wickedness, and cleanse me from my sin.

For I acknowledge my faults, and my sin is ever before me.

Against thee only have I sinned, and done this evil in thy sight that thou mightest be justified in thy saying, and clear when thou art judged.

Behold, I was shapen in wickedness, and in sin hath my mother conceived me.

But lo, thou requirest truth in the inward parts, and shalt make me to understand wisdom secretly.

Thou shalt purge me with hyssop, and I shall be clean; thou shalt wash me, and I shall be whiter than snow.

Thou shalt make me hear of joy and gladness, that the bones which thou hast broken may rejoice.

Turn thy face from my sins, and put out all my misdeeds.

Make me a clean heart, O God, and renew a right spirit within me.

Cast me not away from thy presence, and take not thy holy Spirit from me.

O give me the comfort of thy help again, and stablish me with thy free Spirit.

Then shall I teach thy ways unto the wicked, and sinners shall be converted unto thee.

Deliver me from blood-guiltiness, O God, thou that art the God of my health; and my tongue shall sing of thy righteousness.

Thou shalt open my lips, O Lord, and my mouth shall show thy praise.

For thou desirest no sacrifice, else would I give it to thee; but thou delightest not in burnt-offerings.

The sacrifice of God is a troubled spirit: a broken and contrite heart, O God shalt thou not despise.

Glory be to the Father, and to the Son, and to the Holy Ghost;

As it was in the beginning is now, and ever shall be, world without end. *Amen.*

THE KYRIE

Lord, have mercy upon us.
Christ, have mercy upon us.
Lord, have mercy upon us.

THE LORD'S PRAYER

Our Father who art in heaven, hallowed be thy name; thy kingdom come; thy will be done on earth as it is in heaven. Give us this day our daily bread. And forgive us our trespasses, as we forgive those who trespass against us. And lead us not into temptation, but deliver us from evil. For thine is the kingdom, and the power, and the glory, forever. *Amen.*

THE VERSICLES

O Lord, save thy servants;
That put their trust in thee.
Send unto them help from above.
And evermore mightily defend them.
Help us, O God our Saviour.
And for the glory of thy name deliver us; be merciful to us sinners, for thy Name's sake.
O Lord, hear our prayer.
And let our cry come unto thee.

THE COLLECTS *Let the people join with the minister in prayer.*

O Lord, we beseech thee, mercifully hear our prayers, and spare all those who confess their sins unto thee; that they, whose consciences by sin are accused, by thy merciful pardon may be absolved; through Christ our Lord. *Amen.*

O Most mighty God, and merciful Father, who hast compassion upon all men, and who wouldest not the death of a sinner, but rather that he should turn from his sin, and be saved; mercifully forgive us our trespasses; receive and comfort us, who are grieved and wearied with the burden of our sins. Thy property is always to have mercy; in thee only is there power to forgive sins. Spare us therefore, good Lord, spare thy people, whom thou hast redeemed; enter not into judgment with thy servants; but so turn thine anger from us, who meekly acknowledge our transgressions, and truly repent us of our faults, and so make haste to help us in this world, that we may ever live with thee in the world to come; through Jesus Christ our Lord. *Amen.*

THE ANTHEM *Let the people join with the minister in prayer.*

Turn thou us, O good Lord, and so shall we be turned. Be favourable, O Lord, Be favourable to thy people, who turn to thee in weeping, fasting, and praying. For thou art a merciful God, full of

compassion, long-suffering, and of great pity. Thou sparest when we deserve punishment, and in thy wrath thinkest upon mercy. Spare thy people, good Lord, spare them, and let not thine heritage be brought to confusion. Hear us, O Lord, for thy mercy is great, and after the multitude of thy mercies look upon us; through the merits and mediation of thy blessed Son, Jesus Christ our Lord. *Amen.*

THE PRAYER FOR PARDON *The minister.*

Almighty God, the Father of our Lord Jesus Christ, who wouldest not the death of a sinner, but rather that he may turn from his wickedness and live; thou dost pardon and absolve all them that truly repent and unfeignedly believe thy holy gospel. Wherefore we beseech thee to grant us true repentance, and thy Holy Spirit, that those things may please thee which we do at this present, and that the rest of our living hereafter may be pure and holy, so that at the last we may come to eternal joy; through Jesus Christ our Lord. *Amen.*

THE BENEDICTION *To be said if no other service is to follow.*

The Lord bless us, and keep us. The Lord make his face to shine upon us, and be gracious unto us. The Lord lift up his countenance upon us, and give us peace, both now and evermore. *Amen.*

HOLY COMMUNION

HOLY COMMUNION

A COMMENTARY ON THE METHODIST LITURGY of the Lord's Supper takes on the proportions of a historical study. It is the cumulative histories of successive revisions, abridgments and alterations. Its form and comeliness may have been conceived in the nomadic tents of the Hittites 2000 years before Christ. The badge of its maturity is its long and honored existence "... developed and curtailed, overlaid with superstitions and purged from accretions, assailed with the fiercest bigotry, and defended through good report and evil report . . ." (*The Divine Liturgy,* H. M. Luckock, Longmans, Green, Co.).

Its fruition blossoms in the whispered words of the faithful participant, "Surely the Lord is in this place . . . this is none other than the house of God, and this is the gate of heaven." (Gen. 28:17.)

The passionate embrace of Holy Communion and the ensuing pressure of God upon the communicant is experienced by only a few of Christ's suitors. Much of the historical and spiritual charm of the Lord's Last Supper goes unnoticed from a lack of appreciation and intelligent understanding. To get the fullest measure of devotion and spiritual refreshment we should acquaint ourselves with the pageant of Holy Communion as it unfolds and progresses before our eyes.

Most Methodist Churches follow the instructions of Paragraph 1908 in the 1952 Discipline and use "The Order for the Administration of the Sacrament of the Lord's Supper or Holy Communion I." This order *is* the complete order of worship for those Sundays or any other time when Holy Communion is to be celebrated and it should not be tampered with by self-styled liturgical improvisators.

The first of the five preliminary rubrics suggests that a fair linen cloth should cover the Lord's Table. Ancient usage insists that the linen cloth represents the linen in which Christ was buried. Upon the linen there are often five embroidered crosses, one at each corner and one in the center, drawing continual attention to the five wounds of the Lord upon the cross. Because of the very personal nature of its association with the Lord, the fair linen cloth is often made by hand rather than by machine. In some denominations it is left on the altar at all times.

The second rubric is sufficient unto itself. Most Protestant churches, to be consistent in their fight against the powerful liquor industries, insist on the unfermented juice of the grape, even though wine is more ancient and symbolic. It is interesting to note that the Methodists at Oxford were the first to mix water with wine for their celebrations of the Lord's Supper. Today it is widely practiced by the liturgical churches.

The third rubric reminds the communicant that kneeling is the preferred posture for communing, but standing or sitting is allowed. The posture of the communicant today is a ramification of a theological difference of the seventeenth century.

Bishop William Laud, the Nonjurors, and the supporters of the First Prayer Book of Edward VI, pictured the communion table as an altar and the communion act as an Eucharistic sacrifice. To the Puritans, however, it was merely a table and Holy Communion but a fellowship meal. Those who believed the table to be an altar and the communion act the dramatization of Christ's sacrifice knelt. Those who saw it only as a fellowship meal sat or stood. The Wesleys strongly supported the Laudian theology of the Eucharistic sacrifice and therefore they knelt at Holy Communion. With the seeping of Puritan influence into Wesleyanism the rubric was expanded to include other postures and inadvertently a totally incompatible theology.

The fourth rublic solicits the use of the tools of devotion in preparation for the sacrament. If silent prayer and meditation are not the tools of every expectant communicant, as suggested they should be in the rubric, then his corporate devotions are often rough and unfinished.

The final rubric launches the service by suggesting the first hymn. In Wesley's service there appears a rubric directing the minister to stand at the altar or table. This does seem more in keeping with the mood of the Eucharist. Certainly there seems to be something incongruous about leading the events of the Lord's Last Supper from a pulpit or lectern when the table or altar is an intricate fixture of the remembrance.

To summarize the obvious is to remind ourselves of our laxity toward the Holy Communion rubrics. They may take on the proportions of fly specks on the periphery of spiritual dynamics. Yet they have a purpose and should be considered a part of the total worship scheme. Wesley in his "Earnest Appeal to Men of Reason and Religion," wrote: "In every parish where I have been curate yet, I have observed the rubrics with scrupulous exactness, not for wrath, but for conscience sake." (*The Sacrament of the Lord's Supper in Early Methodism,* John C. Bowner, Dacre Press.)

After the singing of the processional hymn the congregation and minister read responsively the words of adoration. Armed with scripture these sentences unveil before the worshipper the quadrivial nature of God. The sentences are taken from John 4:23, I John 1:7, Isaiah 40:31, and I John 3:1.

The words of adoration did not appear in Wesley's Sunday Service nor in the succeeding revisions here in America. They first appeared in the 1932 Discipline of the Methodist Episcopal Church. The prefixing of the words of adoration to the Holy Communion liturgy by the 1928 Commission on Ritual and Orders of Worship of the Methodist Episcopal Church was reflective of a growing conviction that we should always come before God with a "joyous song and praises." The theological overtones here are discordant with tradition. Tradition insists that man is unworthy to speak words of praise to God before he has begged God's forgiveness of past misbehavior. There is a certain naïveté about words of adoration preluding the Lord's Supper. It is reminiscent of Robert Browning's:

> The year's at the spring
> And day's at the morn.
> God's in his heaven:
> All's right with the world.

Considering the present world outlook it might be more realistic to prelude our services with the Psalmist's:

> Worship the Lord in holy array;
> tremble before him, all the earth!

Perhaps the words of adoration and the Gloria Patri would rest more comfortable in their foremost position if they were thought of more as a choral introit to worship.

Historically Holy Communion has been divided into three distinct parts: ante-communion, communion, and post-communion. Ante-communion was the period of instruction preceding the act of communion which was open to the neophyte and baptized alike. During this period the Decalogue and creeds and scripture were rehearsed and recited until the unbaptized knew by rote the basic laws and commandments of this new faith. When the instruction and exposition was completed by the leader the unbaptized would leave and the love feast or *agape* would begin. Here was enacted the table events of the Lord's Last Supper. Post-communion involved those prayers and hymns which expressed the communicants' thankfulness to the sacrificed Lord.

ANTE-COMMUNION

In the ancient celebration the Lord's Prayer introduced the period of instruction. The Lord's Prayer and Collect for Purity are the only prayers which remain in use today that were part of the priest's vesting preliminaries before Mass in the Sarum Missal.

Wesley did not alter this use as it appeared in the English Prayer Book of 1662. His instructions were, "The elder standing at the Table, shall say the Lord's Prayer with the Collect following, the people kneeling." Why the Lord's Prayer and Collect were transposed in the 1932 Discipline is difficult to determine. It may be indicative of a calcified pattern of churchly procedure which demands that the Lord's Prayer be tacked on all prayers and said by all present.

Now that the congregation is invited to rehearse the prayers with the minister this act should be dramatized in all its penitential finery. The Collect serves as an ultra-personal invocation to communion by casting the brilliant light of divine introspection into the deepest and darkest human crevices. The Collect, like the Anglican Call to Confession, outlines the patterns of worship, the need for confession, and introduces the more specific spiritual examinations in the Ten Commandments. The Lord's Prayer at this juncture serves as a prayer for pardon or words of assurance.

The present pattern for the Decalogue Litany dates back to Cranmer. In Cranmer's 1549 revision of the Prayer Book he left unchanged the Latin Mass. Protestant pressure, however, forced him to make changes in the 1552 revision which are still characteristic of English liturgy and also of those Churches such as the

Methodist which have liturgical primogenitures in the English Church. It was at this time that the Ten Commandments with Kyrie response was included after a long absence from the liturgy.

The Commandments, as it has been suggested already, are instructional and penitential in nature. They represent a scrutiny of the soul punctuated with the ancient Kyrie response, "Lord have mercy. . . ." Cranmer intended that the Kyrie would fortify the mood of contrition. The early Christians and pagan Greeks used this same Kyrie, however, as an acclamation of praise. It might either be addressed to Caesar or a god, depending on whose favor and help was more potent at the time. To be in keeping with the tonal qualities of both ancient and medieval moods, the Kyrie should be sung using the arrangement and music on page 575 of *The Methodist Hymnal.* To repeat, "Lord, have mercy upon us, and write all these thy laws in our hearts we beseech Thee," after each commandment as it is written in the Hymnal and Book of Worship is too cumbersome. It is more logical and correct that that particular response come after the last commandment only. "Lord, have mercy upon us, and incline our hearts to keep this law," should be used for all but the last Kyrie response.

Following the Ten Commandments is the Lord's Summary of the Law. This transcript of Matthew 22:37-40 did not appear in the communion office until 1718 when the English Non-jurors disliked the literal interpretation the Puritans placed on the fourth Commandment and also wanted to emphasize the Commandment of Love as the only Law. The Summary of the Law and Decalogue were placed in the Methodist ritual in 1932 along with the words of adoration. Needless to say the Summary of the Law was not included in Wesley's Sunday Service. There is nothing incongruous about the Decalogue or the Summary. One spells out the particulars of devotion; the other describes the feelings of devotion. When seen in the white light of Decalogue and Summary perfection, we crawl with uncleanliness and cry out, "Lord, have mercy upon us. . . ."

The Beatitudes have been added to the Methodist liturgy to augment the other laws by adding a strong note of New Testament authority. Since the Beatitudes do not harmonize too well with the other liturgical material and consume precious time, it is natural for them to be omitted.

The responsive scripture, Isaiah 53:1-10, appeared in the 1939 Discipline at the Uniting Conference in deference to the Methodist Protestant Church where it was used regularly. The responsive scripture predicts the Good Friday events. While it does not clash with the sombre color scheme of Holy Communion, it is of a slightly different texture and along with the Beatitudes should be omitted.

With the reading of the Epistle and Gospel ante-communion drops its penitential prelude and quickly assumes the full role of instructor. Of course the readings selected should still reflect the good news of salvation to all who are penitent and obedient under the Law of Christ.

If an anthem is to be sung it should separate the Epistle and Gospel. The use of music between the Epistle and Gospel dates back to early celebrations of the Eucharist. To the primordial liturgists the reading of the Gospel was the climax of the ante-communion. After the Epistle reading a deacon would carry the Gospel book from the altar to the pulpit while the cantor chanted a psalm. (This was called the Gradual from the name of the step upon which the cantor stood while chanting *gradus*.) The carrying of the Gospel book, while the congregation stood, symbolized the bringing of the Gospel from heaven (the altar) to mankind (the pulpit).

It might be well if we would return to the custom of standing for the Gospel, not only because standing usually signifies a gesture of respect and admiration for the Gospel, but in a practical sense the congregation's position is prepared for the reciting of the creed following the Gospel lesson.

For some unknown reason Wesley did not include a creed in his Sunday Service Communion Office. It is certain that he repeated the creed in his own celebration, nor did he possess any theological reservations concerning the use of creeds or the words of any particular creed. Wesley was led, however, by a desire to compress the English rite for American approval. The creed apparently fell victim to his compressions. The Methodist Episcopal Church, South, was the first Church to reinstate the creed. At present it is permitted, but the mechanics of hunting through the Hymnal or Book of Worship is a great deterrent to its use.

The Nicene Creed has been historically associated with Holy Communion. It was first recited as a part of the Holy Communion celebration the year 473. The recitation was ordered by Patriarch Peter the Fuller of Antioch. The Creed was used to clearly delimit the nature of Christ. Arianism during the reign of Constantine had influenced many to believe that Christ was not the only begotten son of God (*homoousion*), but that Christ was only the word of God. At the Council of Nicaea in 325 the nature of Christ was indelibly stamped with the words: "very God of very God, begotten not made, of one substance."

Therefore, one hundred years later the Nicene Creed was used at the Eucharist to distinguish between those who believed in the dual nature of Christ and those who denied it. The Nicene Creed is used today at Holy Communion because of continuing emphasis upon the offering of God in the form of Jesus Christ for the sins of the world. It is also used because it is a statement of orthodox Christianity and, therefore, fits well into the historic framework of the Holy Communion liturgy.

Contrary to common practice, there should by all means be a sermon. In fact Holy Communion in many Prayer Books is the only office which provides for a sermon. Here is a great opportunity to close the period of instruction with a prophetic voice mingled with the voices of centuries past.

The two rubrics preceding the offertory sentences are all that is left in Methodist practice of the beautiful and symbolic liturgy of the Medieval Church. The instruction to remove the linen cloth from the elements while the congregation is singing a hymn is but a shadow of the past glories that surrounded the bringing of the sacrificial gifts of money, bread, and wine.

In the first four centuries of the Christian celebration the people themselves brought bread and wine along with their money offerings. This incidentally placed a great burden on their conscience. Giving the elements, representing Christ's sacrifice, for the Eucharist, the people were reminded that their gift of money should constitute a sacrifice. And often it was. After the fourth century the Eastern Church and eventually the English Church developed the Great

Entrance. This was a procession of laymen who brought the oblations of money, bread, and wine to the altar while the rest of the congregation chanted a Psalm or the offertory sentences.

Those who have attended a dramatic production at a "theatre-in-the-round" know how effectively the audience feels a part of the plot when entrances and exits must be made down the aisles to the stage. In the same way we might profitably incorporate the Great Entrance into our Communion services. This should cause the congregation to feel more involved in the sacrificial drama and Christ's own offering to all peoples. Seeing the elements at the head of the procession, memorable of Christ's walk to the cross might also cause a parsimonious congregation to exuviate their niggardliness and make some sacrificial offering to the ushers. This could all be done while the congregation is singing, "All things come of thee, O Lord. . . ."

Following the response is David's offertory prayer from I Chronicles 29:11, 12. David was reflecting the joy of the Hebrews at their willingness to give for the building of the Temple. In the Anglican rite the Prayer of the Church comes at this juncture. Wesley included a Prayer for the Church Militant in his Sunday Service but it was omitted here in America in 1792. David's prayer or exclamation concludes ante-communion.

COMMUNION

Now the atmosphere of Holy Communion grows heavy with the accelerated intensity of the portrayal of the actual table events of the Lord's Last Supper. It is to the faithful of God's Kingdom that the command, "draw near" is lovingly directed. The Invitation is reminiscent of celebrations in the medieval cathedral. After the unconfirmed had been dismissed the confirmed would gather in the choir where they would be nearer the sacrament activities. The Invitation as we now use it first appeared in the 1552 Prayer Book and was composed by Cranmer from much older sources.

The Invitation should leave no doubt in the communicant's mind about his spiritual preparation for communion. Repentance, love, and faith must inundate all other emotions before we can "take this Holy Sacrament." Our leading a "new life" depends totally upon the extent to which we flood ourselves with this trinity of devotion.

The rubric directing the minister to kneel and lead the congregation in the General Confession seems almost unnecessary at this point. The Invitation is the rubric *par excellence*. Nothing is left for us to do but to kneel and confess "The heinousness of our sin, in whichever of its forms—'thought, word, and deed . . .' " that keeps us from perfect communion with God and His Son Jesus Christ. (The total impact of this prayer of confession is best achieved on one's knees.) Massey Shepard, *The Oxford American Prayer Book Commentary*. Wesley, following the 1552 Prayer Book, instructed only the minister or a member of the congregation to intone this prayer. To the credit of later redactors, all may now participate.

The preamble of the Absolution, prayer for pardon, once more reminds us of the prerequisites of God's forgiveness, "hearty repentance and true faith." To the penitent the Absolution sings a heavenly benediction of eternal goodness and everlasting life. Wesley's major change in the Absolution was to substitute "us" for "you." This perhaps was done in deference to the benedictional qualities of the pronouncement and certainly in consideration of his army of lay preachers who would be reciting the declaration.

The Comfortable Words give scriptural support to the Absolution. (I John 2:1, 2; I Timothy 1:15; John 3:16; Matthew 11:28.) Only the arrangement of the sentences has been altered since Wesley's revision. They stand as flying buttresses, arching the gap of time, a voice from the past, supporting and holding firm the meditations made by man.

The Sursum Corda derives its name from the first line of the first versicle, "Lift up your hearts." It is impossible to establish a date for its first usage in the liturgy of the Holy Table. It was probably used from the very beginning to introduce the Prayer of Consecration. The first pair of versicles was shouted by the early Christians to condition their minds and souls to the lofty spheres of the spiritual banquet. The second pair of versicles is the Jewish benediction over the cup of blessing at the common meal. Its appropriateness at this juncture is unchallenged. The Comfortable Words and Sursum Corda have been restored to the Methodist liturgy in the last twenty-five years after an absence of over one hundred years. Previous to the restoration, the Collect for Purity followed the Absolution.

The Introduction to the Prefaces and the Prefaces themselves appeared in all the Prayer Books after 1549. They were included in Wesley's Sunday Service and in Methodist liturgy until 1924. In the 1924 Discipline The Introduction to the Prefaces and the Prefaces were placed *after* the communication of the ministers. They continued to be out of joint until they were reset in their normal position by the Commission on Rituals for the 1932 Discipline. The Introduction to the Prefaces and the Prefaces to the Sanctus inject a unique quality to Christian worship. The Introduction to the Prefaces strongly hints that the occasion for the worship of God should not be subject to the whims of the individual but that "at all times and in all places (we should) give thanks. . . ." For, as the Sanctus suggests, we not only worship with other earthlings but "with the whole company of heaven, evermore praising thee, and saying, Holy, holy, holy, Lord God of hosts, heaven and earth are full of thy glory. Glory be to thee, O Lord most high! Amen."

The Sanctus was the great "Seraphic Hymn" heard by Isaiah in the Temple. It was used in the liturgy of the Jewish synagogue and later found its way into early Christian practices. If the mood is to be ventilated properly, the Sanctus must be sung. It is interesting to note that the 1928 Discipline gave the page number for the music to be used with the Santus. In the 1928 Ritual the Preface and Sanctus followed the minister's communion and preceded the people's communion. A similar condition existed in the Ritual of the Methodist Episcopal Church, South, as late as 1938. Here the Preface and Sanctus followed the Collect for Purity, which appeared where the Comfortable Words are normally placed. The Sursum Corda, which logically introduces the Introduction of the Prefaces, was omitted. (Last line of Sursum Corda, "It is meet and right so to do." First line of Introduction to the Prefaces, "It is very meet, right. . . .") For some reason in this same service the Lord's Prayer separated the minister's communion and the people's communion.

Actually the Prayer of Consecration begins with the Sursum Corda and ends with the Thanksgiving in the Post-communion. The foundation for the Prayer of Consecration was laid by the Jews. It was customary for the Hebrew host to utter a prayer of thanksgiving over the "cup of blessing" at the conclusion of the common meal.

The prayer contained three basic themes: 1, a thanksgiving for the food and all other benefits; 2, a thanksgiving for the covenant of redemption God made with the Jews; 3, a prayer for the gathering together of all the faithful into the everlasting Kingdom of God. Even without a complete study of the Prayer of Consecration it can be seen that the early Christians borrowed the pattern for their prayer from the Thanksgiving at the end of the common meal.

Immediately following Christ's death and for the next 300 years the exact wording of the Prayer of Consecration was left to the vocal prowess of the celebrant. During the fourth century, however, the Prayer of Consecration was formalized and furnished with an outline of moods which, with one or two major exceptions, has defied the tamperings of liturgical redactors. The outline for the Prayer is as follows: (Keep in mind the previously mentioned boundaries of the Prayer.) 1. The Preface, a hymn of praise to the Father of Christ, in which we join with the angels and archangels to magnify the holiness of the Lord. 2. The Prayer of Consecration proper; here we praise God for the sacrificial giving of His Son for our salvation, which is recalled to us through the Words of Institution at the closing of the Prayer. 3. The Oblation or offering of the holy gifts of bread and wine to God. In the Second Prayer Book of Edward VI, 1661, the Oblation was called the First Thanksgiving and it followed immediately after the act of communion. The prayer was misplaced. Wesley did not change the position, although he did delete the second Thanksgiving, probably to shorten the service. The Oblation or First Thanksgiving should follow the Prayer of Consecration. The prayer mood is anticipatory, preparing the communicant for the act of communion. The American Book of Common Prayer has restored the Oblation to its rightful position immediately following the Prayer of Consecration.

4. The next in the historic outline is the Invocation. This prayer has been deleted in its entirety by Wesley and succeeding Methodists. In the Roman Mass it is the Prayer of Invocation which turns the elements of bread and wine into the actual body and blood of Christ. Obviously it is omitted from most Protestant services, and where it is used the accent is entirely different from that

of the Roman transubstantiation. 5. The Prayer of Humble Access follows the Invocation. The Prayer Book of 1661 placed the Prayer of Humble Access before the Prayer of Consecration. Not until the 1932 Discipline did the Prayer of Humble Access return to its ancient position. 6. The final sequence in the act of Consecration was the Lord's Prayer. Wesley placed the Prayer after the act of communion. Since the Lord's Prayer is repeated earlier in the service, it has been omitted from this section. The Methodist Episcopal Church, South, at the time of the Uniting Conference, still included the Lord's Prayer.

Our present Prayer of Consecration proper is most similar in wording to that of the Scottish Communion Office of 1764. As has been already noted, it contains two separate thoughts. At the beginning we are reminded of the sacrifice of Christ and our obligation to continue its remembrance, while at its conclusion there is a rehearsal of the words of Christ instituting and giving scriptural authority to the memorial feast.

The Manual Acts suggested by footnotes in the Prayer of Consecration should be observed since they make the words visible and symbolically dramatic. In the lifting of the cup by the minister there need be no fear of the act's representing the elevating of the Host by the Catholic priest. It is merely word imagery.

The Prayer of Humble Access is the last desperate plea to God that our total unworthiness might be covered by His grace before we become partakers of "these memorials." The Prayer beautifully and completely expresses the hope of all true Christians that we who partake of these memorials of Jesus Christ, "may be filled with the fullness of his life, may grow into his likeness, and may evermore dwell in him, and he in us."

The act of communion should be unhurried and at the communion or altar rail, with the people kneeling. The posture for communion has already been explained. Those ministers who allow the ushers to "serve" the elements to a seated congregation prostitute the memory of John Wesley. While this in itself may cause no pains of remorse, certainly the impersonal and geographic impossibility for those sincerely wishing to kneel might cause questions of procedure to arise in the nonconforming elder's mind.

It is said that an ancient custom of nomadic peoples was to

offer sanctuary to friend or enemy alike in one's tent. The modern nomad still repeats the ageless formula of hospitality to his guest while serving the final cup. "This is my blood, drink all of it, and while it remains in your body, you are under my protection." Could it have been that Christ was paraphrasing this nomadic pronouncement to assure his continual presence with his disciples in words that they were familiar and potent to them.

In any event these words repeated to the communicant while kneeling and at the moment he touches the memorials of Christ's body are the ultimate in personal devotionalism. The words, "This is my body and blood given for you," should produce a soulquake which can only be repaired by ever-increasing love and devotion to Christ.

POST-COMMUNION

The Prayer of Thanksgiving introduces the Post-communion prayers. The Thanksgiving or Eucharist, as some denominations interpret it, has previously been alluded to in reference to the Oblation. A layman's definition of Oblation is: to offer something, make an offering. In this Prayer the communicant is offering himself to the service of God's Kingdom. Sinful, unworthy, unfit though we may be, it is our bounden duty as disciples to leave the holy table and hallowed objects and practice our revived devotion out in the world of men, machines, and institutions.

The final hymn is always the Gloria in Excelsis; no other hymn is necessary; no other hymn can match its beauty and majesty. It should by all or any means be sung. There is no suitable reason why after practice and patience the congregation and choir cannot join with the minister and "sing unto the Lord with thanksgiving."

The Gloria in Excelsis inherits its comeliness from the ancient Messianic praise-shouts of the Jews. Its body is constructed of the early confessions of the Christian faith. To sing with organ, choir, and congregation is the only way this great hymn of the Christian Church can best be expressed.

The blessing is an expansion of Philippians 4:7. Originally it was pronounced at the close of Ante-communion. Cranmer, however, placed it in its present position and with the present wording. The prayer recognizes the inability of man to grasp all the mysteries of the sacrament, but the presence and peace of God will find a way to make mankind intelligent and ardent suitors of Jesus Christ.

> Grant we beseech thee, O Lord, to thy faithful people, that they may both continually receive the paschal sacraments, and earnestly look forward to that which is approaching; so that steadfastly abiding in the mysteries by which they have been renewed, they may by this means be brought to newness of life.
>
> SARUM MISSAL.

HOLY COMMUNION

Adapted from

THE SUNDAY SERVICE OF JOHN WESLEY

The Lord's Table should have upon it a fair linen cloth.

Let the pure, unfermented juice of the grape be used.

It is our custom to receive the Sacrament of the Lord's Supper kneeling, but if persons so desire, they may receive the elements while seated or standing.

Upon entering the church let the communicants bow in prayer and in the spirit of prayer and meditation approach the blessed Sacrament.

The people shall stand and join in singing the hymn, "Holy, holy, holy, Lord God Almighty," or other suitable hymn, and remain standing until after the singing of the Gloria Patri.

PROCESSIONAL HYMN

WORDS OF ADORATION

God is a Spirit. They that worship him must worship him in spirit and in truth. (John 4:23.)

Glory be to God on high.

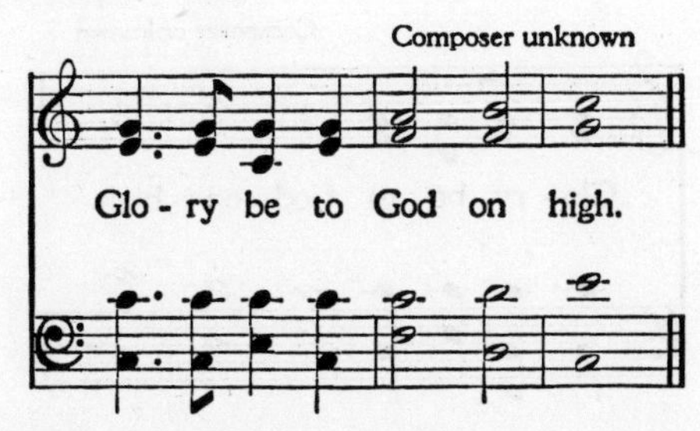
Composer unknown
Glo - ry be to God on high.

God is Light. If we walk in the light, as he is in the light, we have fellowship one with another; and truly our fellowship is with the Father, and with his Son Jesus Christ. (I John 1:7.)

Glory be to God on high.

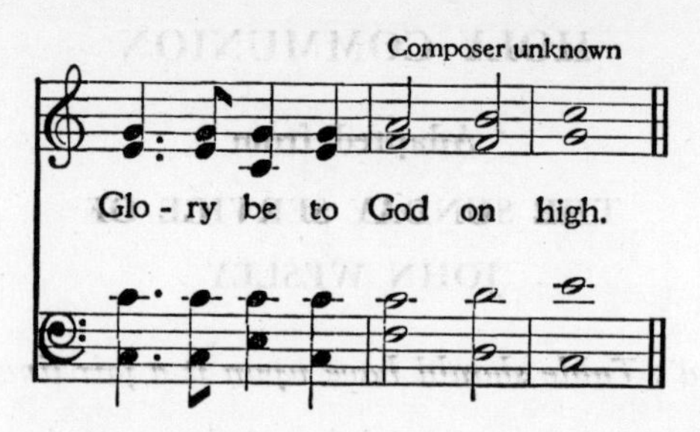

God is power. They that wait upon the Lord shall renew their strength; they shall mount up with wings as eagles; they shall run, and not be weary; and they shall walk, and not faint. (Isaiah 40:31.)

Glory be to God on high.

God is Love. Behold, what manner of love the Father hath bestowed upon us, that we should be called the sons of God. Hereby preceive we the love of God, because he laid down his life for us. I John 3:1.

Glory be to God on high.

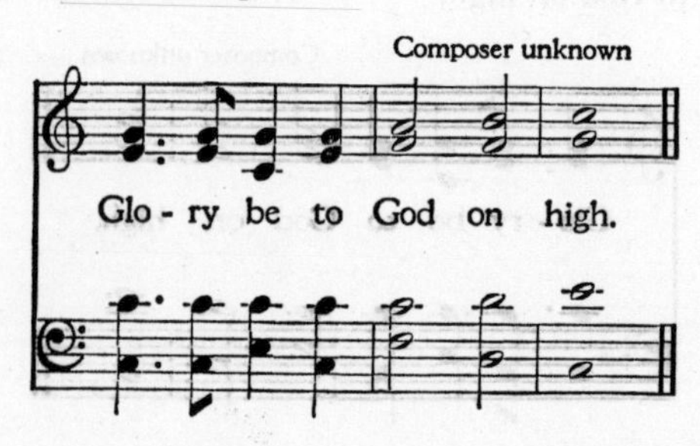

GLORIA PARTI *To be said or sung.*

Glory be to the Father, and to the Son, and to the Holy Ghost; as it was in the beginning, is now, and ever shall be, world without end. *Amen.*

(Then shall the minister say:)

Let us pray.

Collect for Purity

Almighty God, unto whom all hearts are open, all desires known, and from whom no secrets are hid; cleanse the thoughts of our hearts by the inspiration of thy Holy Spirit, that we may perfectly love thee, and worthily magnify thy holy name; through Jesus Christ our Lord. *Amen.*

Lord's Prayer

Our Father who art in heaven, hallowed be thy name; thy kingdom come; thy will be done on earth as it is in heaven. Give us this day our daily bread. And forgive us our trespasses, as we forgive those who trespass against us. And lead us not into temptation, but deliver us from evil. For thine is the kingdom, and the power, and the glory, forever. *Amen.*

Then may the minister read the Ten Commandments, and the people, still in the attitude of prayer, shall in response ask God's mercy for their transgressions in times past and grace to keep the law in time to come.

The Ten Commandments

God spake these words and said: I am the Lord thy God: thou shalt have no other gods before me.

Lord, have mercy upon us, and incline our hearts to keep this law.

Thomas Tallis, c. 1520–1585

May be sung after each Commandment except the tenth

Lord, have mer-cy up - on us, and in-cline our hearts to keep this law.

Thou shalt not make unto thee any graven image, or any likeness of anything that is in heaven above, or that is in the earth beneath, or that is in the water under the earth; thou shalt not bow down thyself to them, nor serve them.

Lord, have mercy upon us, and incline our hearts to keep this law.

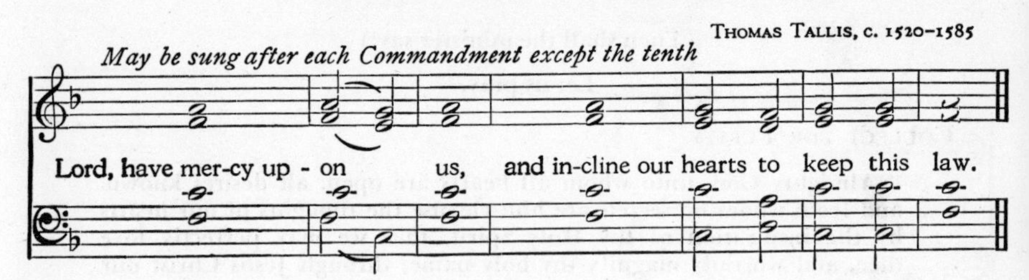

Thou shalt not take the Name of the Lord thy God in vain.

Lord, have mercy upon us, and incline our hearts to keep this law.

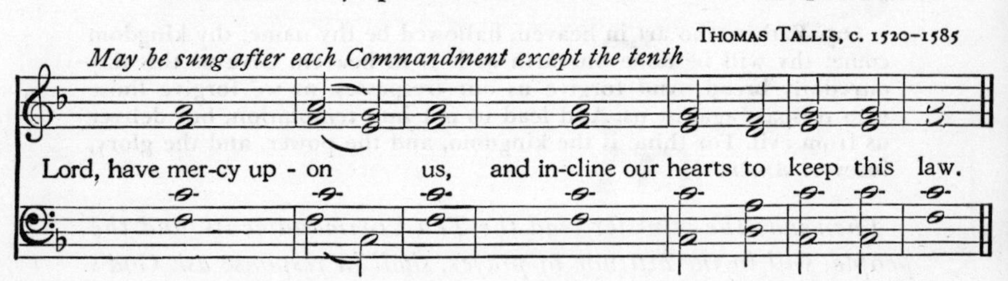

Remember the Sabbath day to keep it holy. Six days shalt thou labor, and do all thy work: but the seventh is the Sabbath of the Lord thy God.

Lord, have mercy upon us, and incline our hearts to keep this law.

Honor thy father and thy mother.

Lord, have mercy upon us, and incline our hearts to keep this law.

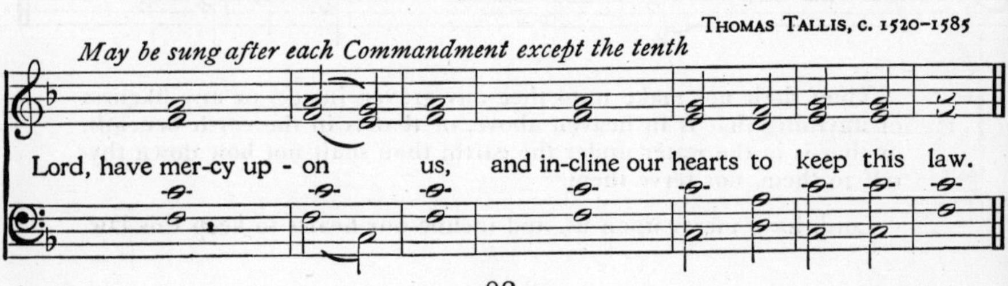

Thou shalt not kill.

Lord, have mercy upon us, and incline our hearts to keep this law.

THOMAS TALLIS, c. 1520–1585

May be sung after each Commandment except the tenth

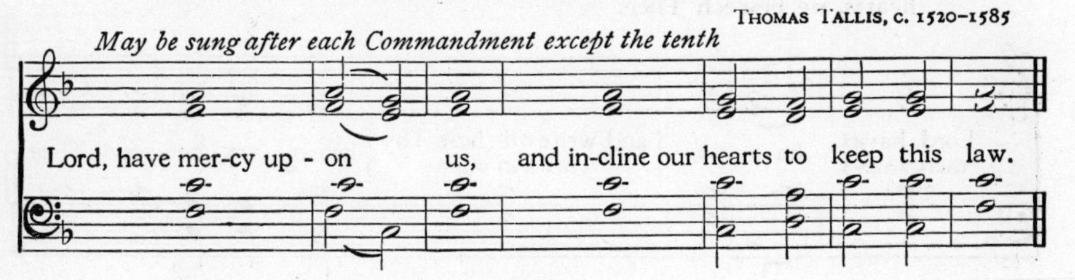
Lord, have mer-cy up - on us, and in-cline our hearts to keep this law.

Thou shalt not commit adultery.

Lord, have mercy upon us, and incline our hearts to keep this law.

THOMAS TALLIS, c. 1520–1585

May be sung after each Commandment except the tenth

Lord, have mer-cy up - on us, and in-cline our hearts to keep this law.

Thou shalt not steal.

Lord, have mercy upon us, and incline our hearts to keep this law.

THOMAS TALLIS, c. 1520–1585

May be sung after each Commandment except the tenth

Lord, have mer-cy up - on us, and in-cline our hearts to keep this law.

Thou shalt not bear false witness.

Lord, have mercy upon us, and incline our hearts to keep this law.

THOMAS TALLIS, c. 1520–1585

May be sung after each Commandment except the tenth

Lord, have mer-cy up - on us, and in-cline our hearts to keep this law.

Thou shalt not covet.

Lord, have mercy upon us, and write all these Thy laws in our hearts, we beseech Thee.

Lord, have mercy up-
on
us,
and write all these Thy laws in our
hearts,
we
be - seech Thee.

OUR LORD'S SUMMARY OF THE LAW

Our Lord Jesus Christ said: the first of all the commandments is, Hear, O Israel; the Lord our God is one Lord: And thou shalt love the Lord thy God with all thy heart, and with all thy soul, and with all thy mind, and with all thy strength: this is the first commandment.

Lord, have mercy upon us, and incline our hearts to keep this law.

THOMAS TALLIS, c. 1520–1585

May be sung after each Commandment except the tenth

Lord, have mer-cy up - on
us,
and in-cline our hearts to
keep
this
law.

And the second is like, namely, this, Thou salt love thy neighbor as thyself.

Lord, have mercy upon us, and incline our hearts to keep this law.

THOMAS TALLIS, c. 1520–1585

May be sung after each Commandment except the tenth

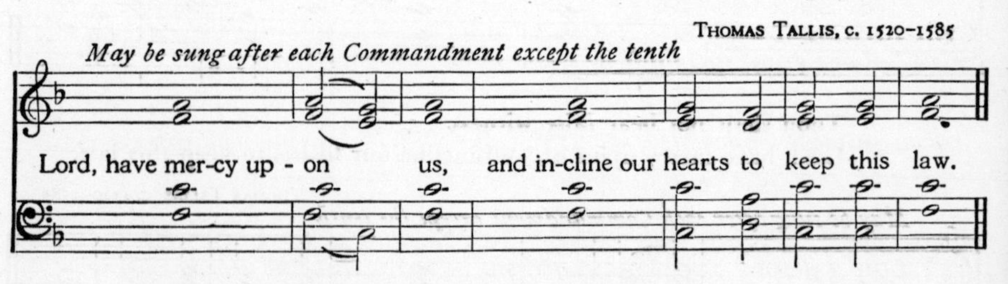
Lord, have mer-cy up - on
us,
and in-cline our hearts to
keep
this
law.

A new commandment I give unto you, That ye love one another; as I have loved you, that ye also love one another.

Lord, have mercy upon us, and write all these Thy laws in our hearts, we beseech Thee.

Lord, have mercy up-
on
us,
and write all these Thy laws in our
hearts,
we
be - seech Thee.

Then may the minister read the Epistle, to be followed by the Gospel.

Here may the minister and people repeat the Creed, the people standing.

Nicene Creed

I believe in one God the Father Almighty, Maker of heaven and earth, and of all things visible and invisible:

And in one Lord Jesus Christ, the only-begotten Son of God, begotten of his Father before all worlds, God of God, Light of Light, very God of very God, begotten not made, being of one substance with the Father, by whom all things were made; who for us men and for our salvation came down from heaven, and was incarnate by the Holy Spirit of the Virgin Mary, and was made man, and was crucified also for us under Pontius Pilate; he suffered and was buried, and the third day he rose again according to the Scriptures, and ascended into heaven, and sitteth on the right hand of the Father; and he shall come again with glory, to judge both the quick and dead, whose kingdom shall have no end.

And I believe in the Holy Spirit, the Lord and Giver of life, who proceedeth from the Father and the Son, who with the Father and the Son together is worshiped and glorified, who spake by the prophets. And I believe one catholic and apostolic Church. I acknowledge one baptism for the remission of sins. And I look for the resurrection of the dead, and the life of the world to come. *Amen.*

Then may follow the sermon or communion meditation and a suitable hymn. During the singing of this hymn the minister shall remove the linen cloth that covers the elements.

After the hymn has been sung, the minister, standing by the Lord's Table, shall announce the offering for the needy, using one or more of the following groups of sentences.

THE OFFERING

I

Remember the words of the Lord Jesus, how he said, It is more blessed to give than to receive. Acts 20:35.

Let your light so shine before men, that they may see your good works, and glorify your Father which is in heaven. Matt. 5:16.

Not everyone that saith unto me, Lord, Lord, shall enter into the kingdom of heaven; but he that doeth the will of my Father which is in heaven. Matt. 7:21.

And the King shall answer and say unto them, Verily I say unto you, Inasmuch as ye have done it unto one of the least of these my brethren, ye have done it unto me. Matt. 25:40.

Therefore all things whatsoever ye would that men should do to you, do ye even so to them: for this is the law and the prophets. Matt. 7:12.

II

Lay not up for yourselves treasures upon earth, where moth and rust doth corrupt, and where thieves break through and steal: but lay up for yourselves treasures in heaven, where neither moth nor rust doth corrupt, and where thieves do not break through nor steal. Matt. 6:19, 20.

He that soweth little shall reap little; and he that soweth plenteously shall reap plenteously. Let every man do according as he is disposed in his heart, not grudgingly, or of necessity; for God loveth a cheerful giver. II Cor. 9:6, 7.

While we have time, let us do good unto all men; and especially unto them that are of the household of faith. Gal. 6:10.

III

Whoso hath this world's good, and seeth his brother have need, and shutteth up his compassion from him, how dwelleth the love of God in him? I John 3:17.

Jesus said unto them, The harvest truly is plenteous, but the laborers are few: pray ye therefore the Lord of the harvest, that he send forth laborers into his harvest. Luke 10:2.

Ye shall not appear before the Lord empty; every man shall give as he is able, according to the blessing of the Lord thy God which he hath given thee. Deut. 16:16, 17.

Thine, O Lord, is the greatness, and the power, and the glory, and the victory, and the majesty: for all that is in the heaven and in the earth is thine; thine is the kingdom, O Lord, and thou art exalted as head above all. I Chron. 29:11.

As the minister receives the offering, the people shall stand, and the following may be said or sung:

All things come of thee, O Lord, and of thine own have we given thee.

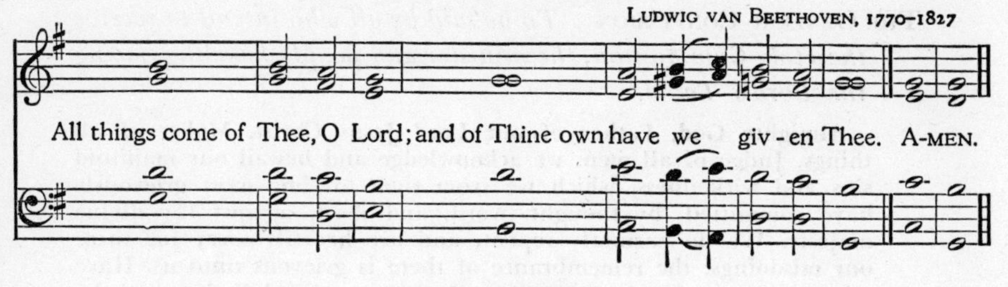
LUDWIG VAN BEETHOVEN, 1770–1827
All things come of Thee, O Lord; and of Thine own have we giv - en Thee. A-MEN.

(or the Doxology)

Praise God from whom all blessings flow; Praise Him, all creatures here below; Praise Him above, ye heavenly host: Praise Father, Son, and Holy Ghost.

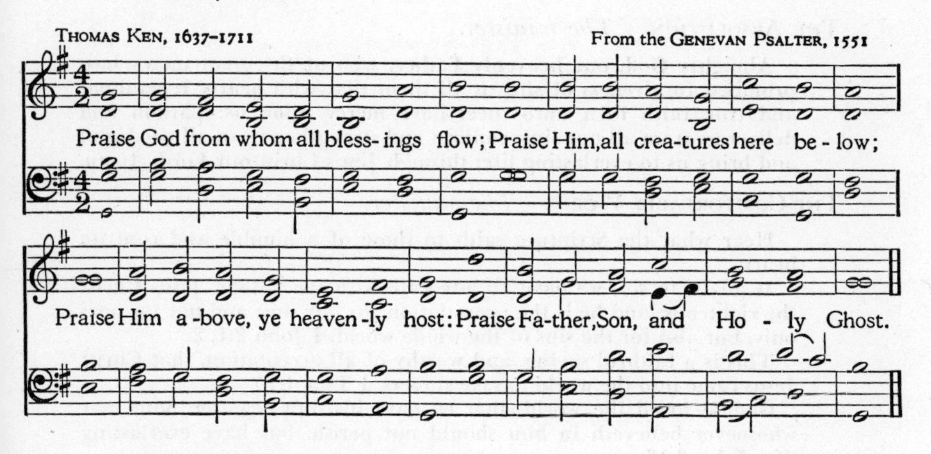
THOMAS KEN, 1637–1711
From the GENEVAN PSALTER, 1551
Praise God from whom all bless- ings flow; Praise Him, all crea-tures here be - low;
Praise Him a -bove, ye heaven -ly host: Praise Fa-ther, Son, and Ho - ly Ghost.

Then shall the minister say:

Thine, O Lord, is the greatness, and the power, and the glory, and the victory, and the majesty; for all that is in the heaven and in the earth is thine; thine is the kingdom, O Lord, and thou art exalted as head above all.

THE INVITATION *The people shall remain standing while the minister reads the invitation.*

Ye that do truly and earnestly repent of your sins, and are in love and charity with your neighbors, and intend to lead a new life, following the commandments of God, and walking from henceforth in his holy ways; draw near with faith, and take this holy Sacrament to your comfort; and devoutly kneeling make your humble confession to Almighty God.

THE GENERAL CONFESSION *To be said by all who intend to receive the Holy Communion, the minister and people kneeling, facing the Lord's Table.*

Almighty God, Father of our Lord Jesus Christ, Maker of all things, Judge of all men; we acknowledge and bewail our manifold sins and wickedness, which we from time to time most grievously have committed, by thought, word, and deed, against thy divine majesty. We do earnestly repent, and are heartily sorry for these our misdoings; the remembrance of them is grievous unto us. Have mercy upon us, have mercy upon us, most merciful Father; for thy Son our Lord Jesus Christ's sake, forgive us all that is past; and grant that we may ever hereafter serve and please thee in newness of life, to the honor and glory of thy name; through Jesus Christ our Lord. *Amen.*

THE ABSOLUTION *The minister.*

Almighty God, our heavenly Father, who of thy great mercy hast promised forgiveness of sins to all them that with hearty repentance and true faith turn unto thee; have mercy upon us; pardon and deliver us from all our sins; confirm and strengthen us in all goodness; and bring us to everlasting life; through Jesus Christ our Lord. *Amen.*

THE COMFORTABLE WORDS *The minister.*

Hear what the Scripture saith to those of a humble and contrite heart:

If any man sin, we have an advocate with the Father, Jesus Christ the righteous: and he is the propitiation for our sins: and not for ours only, but also for the sins of the whole world. I John 2:1, 2.

This is a faithful saying, and worthy of all acceptation, that Christ Jesus came into the world to save sinners. I Tim. 1:15.

God so loved the world, that he gave his only-begotten Son, that whosoever believeth in him should not perish, but have everlasting life. John 3:16.

Come unto me, all ye that labor and are heavy laden, and I will give you rest. Matt. 11:28.

THE SURSUM CORDA *To be said or sung, the minister and people responsively.*

Lift up your hearts.
We lift them up unto the Lord.
Let us give thanks unto the Lord.
It is meet and right so to do.

THE INTRODUCTION TO THE PREFACE *The minister, still kneeling facing the Lord's Table.*

It is very meet, right, and our bounden duty that we should at all times and in all places give thanks unto thee, O Lord, holy Father, almighty, everlasting God.

THE PREFACE *To be said or sung by minister and people.*

Therefore with angels and archangels, and with all the company of heaven, we laud and magnify thy glorious name, evermore praising thee, and saying:

THE SANCTUS

Holy, holy, holy, Lord God of hosts, heaven and earth are full of thy glory. Glory be to thee, O Lord most high! ***Amen.***

Ev - er - more prais - ing Thee, and say - ing: Ho - ly, ho - ly,
ho - ly Lord God of Hosts, Heaven and earth are full of Thy
glo - ry: Glo - ry be to Thee, O Lord, Most High. A - MEN.

PRAYER OF CONSECRATION *The minister, facing the Lord's Table.*

Almighty God, our heavenly Father, who of thy tender mercy didst give thine only Son Jesus Christ to suffer death upon the cross for our redemption; who made there, by the one offering of himself, a full, perfect, and sufficient sacrifice for the sins of the whole world; and did institute, and in his holy gospel command us to continue, this memorial of his precious death: hear us, O merciful Father, we most humbly beseech thee, and grant that we, receiving this bread and wine, according to thy Son our Saviour Jesus Christ's holy institution, in remembrance of his death and passion, may also be partakers of the divine nature through him, who in the same night that he was betrayed took bread;[1] and when he had given thanks, he brake it, and gave it to his disciples, saying, Take, eat; this is my body, which is given for you; do this in remembrance of me. Likewise after supper he took the cup;[2] and when he had given thanks, he gave it to them, saying, Drink ye all of this; for this is my blood of the new covenant which is shed for you, and for many, for the remission of sins; do this, as oft as ye shall drink it, in remembrance of me. *Amen.*

[1] Here may the minister take the plate in his hands.
[2] Here may the minister take the cup in his hands.

PRAYER OF HUMBLE ACCESS *Minister and people, kneeling.*

We do not presume to come to this thy table, O merciful Lord, trusting in our own righteousness, but in thy manifold and great mercies. We are not worthy so much as to gather up the crumbs under thy table. But thou art the same Lord, whose mercy is unfailing. Grant us therefore, gracious Lord, so to partake of these memorials of thy Son Jesus Christ, that we may be filled with the fullness of his life, may grow into his likeness, and may evermore dwell in him, and he in us. *Amen.*

Then shall the minister first receive the Holy Communion in both kinds himself, after which he shall proceed to deliver the same to other ministers in like manner, if any be present. After this, the minister shall administer the Holy Communion to the people, while they are devoutly kneeling.

Before giving the bread, the minister shall say:

Jesus said, "this is my body, which is given for you," Take and eat this in remembrance that Christ died for you, and feed on him in your heart by faith, with thanksgiving.

Before giving the cup, the minister shall say:

Jesus said, "This cup is the new covenant in my blood, which is shed for you." Drink this in remembrance that Christ died for you, and be thankful.

When all have communed, the minister shall place upon the Lord's Table what remains of the consecrated elements, covering the same with the linen cloth. If any of the consecrated elements remain after all have communed, the minister shall dispose of them in a reverent fashion.

THE THANKSGIVING *The minister and people.*

O Lord, our heavenly Father, we, thy humble servants, desire thy fatherly goodness mercifully to accept this our sacrifice of praise and thanksgiving; most humbly beseeching thee to grant that, by the merits and death of thy Son Jesus Christ, and through faith in his blood, we and thy whole Church may obtain forgiveness of our sins, and all other benefits of his passion. And here we offer and present unto thee, O Lord, ourselves, our souls and bodies, to be a reasonable, holy, and living sacrifice unto thee; humbly beseeching thee that all we who are partakers of this Holy Communion may be filled with thy grace and heavenly benediction. And although we be unworthy, through our manifold sins, to offer unto thee any sacrifice, yet we beseech thee to accept this our bounden duty and service; not weighing our merits, but pardoning our offenses; through Jesus Christ our Lord; by whom, and with whom, in the unity of the Holy Spirit, all

honor and glory be unto thee, O Father Almighty, world without end. ***Amen.***

THE GLORIA IN EXCELSIS *To be said or sung by the minister and people, standing.*

Glory be to God on high, and on earth peace, good will toward men. We praise thee, we bless thee, we worship thee, we glorify thee, we give thanks to thee for thy great glory, O Lord God, heavenly King, God the Father Almighty.

O Lord, the only-begotten Son Jesus Christ; O Lord God, Lamb of God, Son of the Father, that takest away the sins of the world, have mercy upon us. Thou that takest away the sins of the world, receive our prayer. Thou that sittest at the right hand of God the Father, have mercy upon us. For thou only art holy; thou only art the Lord; thou only, O Christ, with the Holy Ghost, art most high in the glory of God the Father. ***Amen.***

THE BLESSING *The minister.*

The peace of God, which passeth all understanding, keep your hearts and minds in the knowledge and love of God, and of his Son Jesus Christ our Lord; and the blessing of God Almighty, the Father, the Son, and the Holy Spirit, be among you, and remain with you always. ***Amen.***

PROPER PREFACES

Christmas

Because thou didst give Jesus Christ thine only Son to be born at this time for us, that by taking flesh of our humanity he might make us partakers of the divine glory. Therefore with angels, etc.

Epiphany

Through Jesus Christ our Lord; who, in substance of our mortal flesh, manifested forth his glory, that he might bring us out of darkness into his own glorious light. Therefore with angels, etc.

Easter Day

But chiefly are we bound to praise thee for the glorious resurrection of thy Son Jesus our Lord, who by his death hath destroyed death, and by his rising to life again hath restored to us everlasting life. Therefore with angels, etc.

Whitsunday

Through Jesus Christ our Lord; according to whose most true promise, the Holy Spirit came down as at this time from heaven as a mighty rushing wind and in tongues of fire, whereby we have been brought out of darkness into the clear light and true knowledge of thee, and of thy Son Jesus Christ. Therefore with angels, etc.

THE PSALTER

THE PSALTER

FIRST SUNDAY IN ADVENT

Psalm 50

1. The Mighty One, God the Lord, speaks and summons the earth from the rising of the sun to its setting.
2. Out of Zion, the perfection of beauty, God shines forth.
3. Our God comes, he does not keep silence, before him is a devouring fire, round about him a mighty tempest.
4. He calls to the heavens above and to the earth, that he may judge his people.
5. "Gather to me my faithful ones, who made a covenant with me by sacrifice!"
6. The heavens declare his righteousness, for God himself is judge!
7. "Hear, O my people, and I will speak, O Israel, I will testify against you. I am God, your God.
8. I do not reprove you for your sacrifices; your burnt offerings are continually before me.
9. I will accept no bull from your house, nor he-goat from your folds.
10. For every beast of the forest is mine, the cattle on a thousand hills.
11. I know all the birds of the air, and all that moves in the field is mine.
12. If I were hungry, I would not tell you; for the world and all that is in it is mine.
13. Do I eat the flesh of bulls, or drink the blood of goats?
14. Offer to God a sacrifice of thanksgiving, and pay your vows to the Most High. And call upon me in the day of trouble; I will deliver you, and you shall glorify me."

SECOND SUNDAY IN ADVENT

Psalm 25

1. To thee, O Lord, I lift up my soul.
2. O my God, in thee I trust, let me not be put to shame; let not my enemies exult over me.
3. Yea, let none that wait for thee be put to shame; let them be ashamed who are wantonly treacherous.
4. Make me to know thy ways, O Lord; teach me thy paths.
5. Lead me in thy truth, and teach me, for thou art the God of my salvation; for thee I wait all the day long.
6. Be mindful of thy mercy, O God, and of thy steadfast love, for they have been from of old.
7. Remember not the sins of my youth, or my transgression; according to thy steadfast love remember me, for thy goodness' sake, O Lord!
8. Good and upright is the Lord; therefore he instructs sinners in the way.
9. He leads the humble in what is right, and teaches the humble his way.
10. All the paths of the Lord are steadfast love and faithfulness, for those who keep his covenant and his testimonies.

11. For thy name's sake, O Lord, pardon my guilt, for it is great.
12. Who is the man that fears the Lord? Him will he instruct in the way that he should choose.
13. He himself shall abide in prosperity, and his children shall possess the land.
14. The friendship of the Lord is for those who fear him, and he makes known to them his covenant.
15. My eyes are ever toward the Lord, for he will pluck my feet out of the net.
16. Turn thou to me, and be gracious to me; for I am lonely and afflicted.
17. Relieve the troubles of my heart, and bring me out of my distresses.
18. Consider my affliction and my trouble, and forgive all my sins.
19. Consider how many are my foes, and with what violent hatred they hate me.
20. Oh guard my life, and deliver me; let me not be put to shame, for I take refuge in thee.
21. May integrity and uprightness preserve me, for I wait for thee.
22. Redeem Israel, O God, out of all his troubles.

THIRD SUNDAY IN ADVENT

Psalm 85

1. Lord, thou wast favorable to thy land; thou didst restore the fortunes of Jacob.
2. Thou didst forgive the iniquity of thy people; thou didst pardon all their sin.
3. Thou didst withdraw all thy wrath; thou didst turn from thy hot anger.
4. Restore us again, O God of our salvation, and put away thy indignation toward us!
5. Wilt thou be angry with us for ever? Wilt thou prolong thy anger to all generations?
6. Wilt thou not revive us again, that thy people may rejoice in thee?
7. Show us thy steadfast love, O Lord, and grant us thy salvation.
8. Let us hear what God the Lord will speak, for he will speak peace to his people, to his saints, to those who turn to him in their hearts.
9. Surely his salvation is at hand for those who fear him, that glory may swell in our land.
10. Steadfast love and faithfulness will meet; righteousness and peace will kiss each other.
11. Faithfulness will spring up from the ground, and righteousness will look down from the sky.
12. Yea, the Lord will give what is good, and our land will yield its increase. Righteousness will go before him, and make his footsteps a way.

FOURTH SUNDAY IN ADVENT

Psalm 80

1. Give ear, O Shepherd of Israel, thou who leadest Joseph like a flock! Thou who art enthroned upon the cherubim, shine forth

2. Before E'phraim and Benjamin and Manas'seh! Stir up thy might, and come to save us!

3. Restore us, O God; let thy face shine, that we may be saved!

4. O Lord God of hosts, how long wilt thou be angry with thy people's prayers?

5. Thou hast fed them with the bread of tears, and given them tears to drink in full measure.

6. Thou dost make us the scorn of our neighbors; and our enemies laugh among themselves.

7. Restore us, O God of hosts; let thy face shine, that we may be saved!

8. Thou didst bring a vine out of Egypt; thou didst drive out the nations and plant it.

9. Thou didst clear the ground for it; it took deep root and filled the land.

10. The mountains were covered with its shade, the mighty cedars with its branches;

11. It sent out its branches to the sea, and its shoots to the River.

12. Why then hast thou broken down its walls, so that all who pass along the way pluck its fruit?

13. The boar from the forest ravages it, and all that move in the field feed on it.

14. Turn again, O God of hosts! Look down from heaven, and see; have regard for this vine,

15. The stock which thy right hand planted.

16. They have burned it with fire, they have cut it down; may they perish at the rebuke of thy countenance!

17. But let thy hand be upon the man of thy right hand, the son of man whom thou hast made strong for thyself!

18. Then we will never turn back from thee; give us life, and we will call on thy name! Restore us, O Lord God of hosts! let thy face shine, that we may be saved!

CHRISTMAS DAY

Psalm 89:1-28

1. I will sing of thy steadfast love, O Lord, for ever; with my mouth I will proclaim thy faithfulness to all generations.

2. For thy steadfast love was established for ever, thy faithfulness is firm as the heavens.

3. Thou hast said, "I have made a covenant with my chosen one, I have sworn to David my servant:

4. 'I will establish your descendants for ever, and build thy throne for all generations.' "

5. Let the heavens praise thy wonders, O Lord, thy faithfulness in the assembly of the holy ones!

6. For who in the skies can be compared to the Lord? Who among the heavenly beings is like the Lord,

7. A God feared in the council of the holy ones, great and terrible above all that are round about him?

8. O Lord God of hosts, who is mighty as thou art, O Lord, with thy faithfulness round about thee?

9. Thou dost rule the raging of the sea; when its waves rise, thou stillest them.

10. Thou didst crush Rahab like a carcass, thou didst scatter thy enemies with thy mighty arm.

11. The heavens are thine, the earth also is thine; the world and all that is in it, thou hast founded them.

12. The north and the south, thou hast created them; Tabor and Hermon joyously praise thy name.

13. Thou hast a mighty arm; strong is thy hand, high thy right hand.

14. Righteousness and justice are the foundation of thy throne; steadfast love and faithfulness go before thee.

15. Blessed are the people who know the festal shout, who walk, O Lord, in the light of thy countenance,

16. Who exult in thy name all the day, and extol thy righteousness.

17. For thou art the glory of their strength; by thy favor our horn is exalted.

18. For our shield belongs to the Lord, our king to the Holy One of Israel.

19. Of old thou didst speak in a vision to thy faithful one, and say: "I have set the crown upon one who is mighty, I have exalted one chosen from the people.

20. I have found David, my servant: with my holy oil I have anointed him;

21. So that my hand shall ever abide with him, my arm also shall strengthen him.

22. The enemy shall not outwit him, the wicked shall not humble him.

23. I will crush his foes before him and strike down those who hate him.

24. My faithfulness and my steadfast love shall be with him, and in my name shall his horn be exalted.

25. I will set his hand on the sea and his right hand on the rivers.

26. He shall cry to me, 'Thou art my Father, my God, and the Rock of my salvation.'

27. And I will make him the first-born, the highest of the kings of the earth.

28. My steadfast love I will keep for him for ever, and my covenant will stand firm for him. I will establish his line for ever and his throne as the days of the heavens. . . ."

FIRST SUNDAY AFTER CHRISTMAS

Psalm 145

1. I will extol thee, my God and King, and bless thy name for ever and ever.

2. Every day I will bless thee, and praise thy name for ever and ever.

3. Great is the Lord, and greatly to be praised, and his greatness is unsearchable.

4. One generation shall laud thy works to another, and shall declare thy mighty acts.

5. Of the glorious splendor of thy majesty, and of thy wondrous works, I will meditate.

6. Men shall proclaim the might of thy terrible acts, and I will declare thy greatness.
7. They shall pour forth the fame of thy abundant goodness, and shall sing aloud of thy righteousness.
8. The Lord is gracious and merciful, slow to anger and abounding in steadfast love.
9. The Lord is good to all, and his compassion is over all that he has made.
10. All thy works shall give thanks to thee, O Lord, and all thy saints shall bless thee!
11. They shall speak of the glory of thy kingdom, and tell of thy power,
12. To make known to the sons of men thy mighty deeds, and the glorious splendor of thy kingdom.
13. Thy kingdom is an everlasting kingdom, and thy dominion endures throughout all generation. The Lord is faithful in all his words, and gracious in all his deeds.
14. The Lord upholds all who are falling, and raises up all who are bowed down.
15. The eyes of all look to thee, and thou givest them their food in due season.
16. Thou openest thy hand, thou satisfiest the desire of every living thing.
17. The Lord is just in all his ways, and kind in all his doings.
18. The Lord is near to all who call upon him, to all who call upon him in truth.
19. He fulfils the desire of all who fear him, he also hears their cry, and saves them.
20. The Lord preserves all who love him; but all the wicked he will destroy. My mouth will speak the praise of the Lord, and let all flesh bless his holy name for ever and ever.

SECOND SUNDAY AFTER CHRISTMAS

Psalm 65

1. Praise is due to thee, O God, in Zion; and to thee shall vows be performed,
2. O thou who hearest prayer! To thee shall all flesh come on account of sins.
3. When our transgressions prevail over us, thou dost forgive them.
4. Blessed is he whom thou dost choose and bring near, to dwell in thy courts! We shall be satisfied with the goodness of thy house, thy holy temple!
5. By dread deeds thou dost answer us with deliverance, O God of our salvation, who art the hope of all the ends of the earth, and of the fartherest seas;
6. Who by thy strength hast established the mountains, being girded with might;
7. Who dost still the roaring of the seas, the roaring of their waves, the tumult of the peoples;
8. So that those who swell at earth's farthest bounds are afraid at thy

signs; thou makest the outgoings of the morning and the evening to shout for joy.

9. Thou visitest the earth and waterest it, thou greatly enriches it; the river of God is full of water; thou providest their grain, for so thou has prepared it.

10. Thou waterest its furrows abundantly, settling its ridges, softening it with showers, and blessing its growth.

11. Thou crownest the year with thy bounty; the tracks of thy chariot drip with fatness.

12. The pastures of the wilderness drip, the hills gird themselves with joy, the meadows clothe themselves with flocks, the valleys deck themselves with grain, they shout and sing together for joy.

FIRST SUNDAY AFTER EPIPHANY

Psalm 72

1. Give the king thy justice, O God, and thy righteousness to the royal son!

2. May he judge thy people with righteousness, and thy poor with justice!

3. Let the mountains bear prosperity for the people, and the hills, in righteousness!

4. May he defend the cause of the poor of the people, give deliverance to the needy, and crush the oppressor!

5. May he live while the sun endures, and as long as the moon, throughout all generations!

6. May he be like rain that falls on the mown grass, like showers that water the earth!

7. In his days may righteousness flourish, and peace abound, till the moon be no more!

8. May he have dominion from sea to sea, and from the River to the ends of the earth!

9. May his foes bow down before him, and his enemies lick the dust!

10. May the kings of Tarshish and of the isles render him tribute, may the kings of Sheba and Seba bring gifts!

11. May all kings fall down before him, all nations serve him!

12. For he delivers the needy when he calls, the poor and him who has no helper.

13. He has pity on the weak and the needy, and saves the lives of the needy.

14. From oppression and violence he redeems their life; and precious is their blood in his sight.

15. Long may he live, may gold of Sheba be given to him! May prayer be made for him continually, and blessings invoked for him all the day!

16. May there be abundance of grain in the land; on the tops of the mountains may it wave; may its fruit be like Lebanon; and may men blossom forth from the cities like the grass of the field!

17. May his name endure for ever, his fame continue as long as the sun! May men bless themselves by him, all nations call him blessed!

18. Blessed be the Lord, the God of Israel, who alone does wondrous

things. Blessed be his glorious name for ever; may his glory fill the whole earth! Amen and Amen!

SECOND SUNDAY AFTER EPIPHANY

Psalm 29

1. Ascribe to the Lord, O heavenly beings, ascribe to the Lord glory and strength.
2. Ascribe to the Lord the glory of his name; worship the Lord in holy array.
3. The voice of the Lord is upon the water; the God of glory thunders, the Lord, upon many waters.
4. The voice of the Lord is powerful, the voice of the Lord is full of majesty.
5. The voice of the Lord breaks the cedars, the Lord breaks the cedars of Lebanon.
6. He makes Lebanon to skip like a calf, and Sir'ion like a young wild ox.
7. The voice of the Lord flashes forth flames of fire.
8. The voice of the Lord shakes the wilderness, the Lord shakes the wilderness of Kadesh.
9. The voice of the Lord makes the oaks to whirl, and strips the forests bare; and in his temple all cry, "Glory!"
10. The Lord sits enthroned over the flood; The Lord sits enthroned as king for ever. May the Lord give strength to his people! May the Lord bless his people with peace!

THIRD SUNDAY AFTER EPIPHANY

Psalm 43

1. Vindicate me, O God, and defend my cause against an ungodly people; from deceitful and unjust men deliver me!
2. For thou art the God in whom I take refuge; why hast thou cast me off? Why go I mourning because of the oppression of the enemy?
3. Oh send out thy light and thy truth; let them lead me, let them bring me to thy holy hill and to thy dwelling!
4. Then I will go to the altar of God, to God my exceeding joy; and I will praise thee with the lyre, O God, my God. Why are you cast down, O my soul, and why are you disquieted within me? Hope in God; for I shall again praise him, my help and my God.

FOURTH SUNDAY AFTER EPIPHANY

Psalm 36

1. Transgression speaks to the wicked deep in his heart; there is no fear of God before his eyes.
2. For he flatters himself in his own eyes that his iniquity cannot be found out and hated.
3. The words of his mouth are mischief and deceit; he has ceased to act wisely and do good.

4. He plots mischief while on his bed; he sets himself in a way that is not good; he spurns not evil.

5. Thy steadfast love, O Lord, extends to the heavens, thy faithfulness to the clouds.

6. Thy righteousness is like the mountains of God, thy judgments are like the great deep; man and beast thou savest, O Lord.

7. How precious is thy steadfast love, O God! The children of men take refuge in the shadow of thy wings.

8. They feast on the abundance of thy house, and thou givest them drink from the river of thy delights.

9. For with thee is the fountain of life; in thy light do we see light.

10. O continue thy steadfast love to those who know thee, and thy salvation to the upright of heart!

11. Let not the foot of arrogance come upon me, nor the hand of the wicked drive me away.

12. There the evildoers lie prostrate, they are thrust down, unable to rise.

FIFTH SUNDAY AFTER EPIPHANY

Psalm 112

1. Praise the Lord. Blessed is the man who fears the Lord, who greatly delights in his commandments!

2. His descendants will be mighty in the land; the generation of the upright will be blessed.

3. Wealth and riches are in his house; and his righteousness endures for ever.

4. Light rises in the darkness for the upright; the Lord is gracious, merciful, and righteous.

5. It is well with the man who deals generously and lends, who conducts his affairs with justice.

6. For the righteous will never be moved; he will be remembered for ever.

7. He is not afraid of evil tidings; his heart is firm, trusting in the Lord.

8. His heart is steady, he will not be afraid, until he sees his desire on his adversaries.

9. He has distributed freely, he has given to the poor; his righteousness endures for ever; his horn is exalted in honor.

10. The wicked man sees it and is angry; he gnashes his teeth and melts away; the desire of the wicked man comes to nought.

SIXTH SUNDAY AFTER EPIPHANY

Psalm 138

1. I give thee thanks, O Lord, with my whole heart; before the gods I sing thy praise;

2. I bow down toward thy holy temple and give thanks to thy name for thy steadfast love and thy faithfulness; for thou hast exalted above everything thy name and thy word.

3. On the day I called, thou didst answer me, my strength of soul thou didst increase.

4. All the kings of the earth shall praise thee, O Lord, for they have heard the words of thy mouth;

5. And they shall sing of the ways of the Lord, for great is the glory of the Lord.

6. For though the Lord is high, he regards the lowly; but the haughty he knows from afar.

7. Though I walk in the midst of trouble, thou dost preserve my life; thou dost stretch out thy hand against the wrath of my enemies, and thy right hand delivers me.

8. The Lord will fulfil his purpose for me; thy steadfast love, O Lord, endures for ever. Do not forsake the work of thy hands.

SEPTUAGESIMA SUNDAY

Psalm 121

1. Lift up my eyes to the hills. From whence does my help come?

2. My help comes from the Lord, who made heaven and earth.

3. He will not let your foot be moved, he who keeps you will not slumber.

4. Behold, he who keeps Israel will neither slumber nor sleep.

5. The Lord is your keeper; the Lord is your shade on your right hand.

6. The sun shall not smite you by day, nor the moon by night.

7. The Lord will keep you from all evil; he will keep your life.

8. The Lord will keep your going out and your coming in from this time forth and for evermore.

SEXAGESIMA SUNDAY

Psalm 71:1-19

1. In thee, O Lord, do I take refuge; let me never be put to shame!

2. In thy righteousness deliver me and rescue me; incline thy ear to me, and save me!

3. Be thou to me a rock of refuge, a strong fortress, to save me, for thou art my rock and my fortress.

4. Rescue me, O my God, from the hand of the wicked, from the grasp of the unjust and cruel man.

5. For thou, O Lord, art my hope, my trust, O Lord, from my youth.

6. Upon thee I have leaned from my birth; thou art he who took me from my mother's womb. My praise is continually of thee.

7. I have been as a portent to many; but thou art my strong refuge.

8. My mouth is filled with thy praise, and with thy glory all the day.

9. Do not cast me off in the time of old age; forsake me not when my strength is spent.

10. For my enemies speak concerning me, those who watch for my life consult together, and say,

11. "God has forsaken him; pursue and seize him, for there is none to deliver him."

12. O God, be not far from me; O my God, make haste to help me!

13. May my accusers be put to shame and consumed; with scorn and disgrace may they be covered who seek my hurt.

14. But I will hope continually, and will praise thee yet more and more.

15. My mouth will tell of thy righteous acts, of thy deeds of salvation all the day, for their number is past my knowledge.

16. With the mighty deeds of the Lord God I will come, I will praise thy righteousness, thine alone.

17. O God, from my youth thou hast taught me, and I still proclaim thy wondrous deeds.

18. So even to old age and gray hairs, O God, do not forsake me, till I proclaim thy might to all the generations to come. Thy power and thy righteousness, O God, reach the high heavens. Thou who hast done great things, O God, who is like thee?

QUINQUAGESIMA SUNDAY

Psalm 103

1. Bless the Lord, O my soul; and all that is within me, bless his holy name!

2. Bless the Lord, O my soul, and forget not all his benefits,

3. Who forgives all your iniquity, who heals all your diseases,

4. Who redeems your life from the Pit, who crowns you with steadfast love and mercy,

5. Who satisfies you with good as long as you live so that your youth is renewed like the eagle's.

6. The Lord works vindication and justice for all who are oppressed.

7. He made known his ways to Moses, his acts to the people of Israel.

8. The Lord is merciful and gracious, slow to anger and abounding in steadfast love.

9. He will not always chide, nor will he keep his anger for ever.

10. He does not deal with us according to our sins, nor requite us according to our iniquities.

11. For as the heavens are high above the earth, so great is his steadfast love toward those who fear him;

12. As far as the east is from the west, so far does he remove our transgressions from us.

13. As a father pities his children, so the Lord pities those who fear him.

14. For he knows our frame; he remembers that we are dust.

15. As for man, his days are like grass; he flourishes like a flower of the field;

16. For the wind passes over it, and it is gone, and its place knows it no more.

17. But the steadfast love of the Lord is from everlasting to everlasting upon those who fear him, and his righteousness to children's children,

18. To those who keep his covenant and remember to do his commandments.

19. The Lord has established his throne in the heavens, and his kingdom rules over all.

20. Bless the Lord, O you his angels, you mighty ones who do his word, hearkening to the voice of his word!

21. Bless the Lord, all his hosts, his ministers that do his will!

22. Bless the Lord, all his works, in all places of his dominion. Bless the Lord, O my soul!

ASH WEDNESDAY

Psalm 32

1. Blessed is he whose transgression is forgiven, whose sin is covered.
2. Blessed is the man to whom the Lord imputes no iniquity, and in whose spirit there is no deceit.
3. When I declared not my sin, my body wasted away through my groaning all day long.
4. For day and night thy hand was heavy upon me; my strength was dried up as by the heat of summer.
5. I acknowledged my sin to thee, and I did not hide my iniquity; I said, "I will confess my transgressions to the Lord"; then thou didst forgive the guilt of my sin.
6. Therefore let every one who is godly offer prayer to thee; at a time of distress, in the rush of great waters, they shall not reach him.
7. Thou art a hiding place for me, thou preservest me from trouble; thou dost encompass me with deliverance.
8. I will instruct you and teach you the way you should go; I will counsel you with my eye upon you.
9. Be not like a horse or a mule, without understanding, which must be curbed with bit and bridle, else it will not keep with you.
10. Many are the pangs of the wicked; but steadfast love surrounds him who trusts in the Lord. Be glad in the Lord, and rejoice, O righteous, and shout for joy, all you upright in heart!

FIRST SUNDAY IN LENT

Psalm 62

1. For God alone my soul waits in silence; from him comes my salvation, my fortress; I shall not be greatly moved.
2. He only is my rock and my salvation, my fortress; I shall not be greatly moved.
3. How long will you set upon a man to shatter him, all of you, like a leaning wall, a tottering fence?
4. They only plan to thrust him down from his eminence. They take pleasure in falsehood. They bless with their mouths, but inwardly they curse.
5. For God alone my soul waits in silence, for my hope is from him.
6. He only is my rock and my salvation, my fortress; I shall not be shaken.
7. On God rests my deliverance and my honor; my mighty rock, my refuge is God.
8. Trust in him at all times, O people; pour out your heart before him; God is a refuge for us.
9. Men of low estate are a delusion; in the balances they go up; they are together lighter than a breath.
10. Put no confidence in extortion, set no vain hopes on robbery; if riches increase, set not your heart on them.

11. Once God has spoken; twice have I heard this; that power belongs to God;

12. And that to thee, O Lord, belongs steadfast love. For thou dost requite a man according to his work.

SECOND SUNDAY IN LENT

Psalm 86

1. Incline thy ear, O Lord, and answer me, for I am poor and needy.

2. Preserve my life, for I am godly; save thy servant who trusts in thee.

3. Thou art my God; be gracious to me, O Lord, for to thee do I cry all the day.

4. Gladden the soul of thy servant, for to thee, O Lord, do I lift up my soul.

5. For thou, O Lord, art good and forgiving, abounding in steadfast love to all who call on thee.

6. Give ear, O Lord, to my prayer; hearken to my cry of supplication.

7. In the day of my trouble I call on thee, for thou dost answer me.

8. There is none like thee among the gods, O Lord, nor are there any works like thine.

9. All the nations thou hast made shall come and bow down before thee, O Lord, and shall glorify thy name.

10. For thou art great and doest wondrous things, thou alone art God.

11. Teach me thy way, O Lord, that I may walk in thy truth; unite my heart to fear thy name.

12. I give thanks to thee, O Lord my God, with my whole heart, and I will glorify thy name for ever.

13. For great is thy steadfast love toward me; thou hast delivered my soul from the depths of Sheol.

14. O God, insolent men have risen up against me; a band of ruthless men seek my life, and they do not set thee before them.

15. But thou, O Lord, art a God merciful and gracious, slow to anger and abounding in steadfast love and faithfulness.

16. Turn to me and take pity on me; give thy strength to thy servant, and save the son of thy handmaid. Show me a sign of thy favor, that those who hate me may see and be put to shame because thou, Lord, hast helped me and comforted me.

THIRD SUNDAY IN LENT

Psalm 143

1. Hear my prayer, O Lord; give ear to my supplications! In thy faithfulness answer me, in thy righteousness!

2. Enter not into judgment with thy servant; for no man living is righteous before thee.

3. For the enemy has pursued me; he has crushed my life to the ground; he has made me sit in darkness like those long dead.

4. Therefore my spirit faints within me; my heart within me is appalled.

5. I remember the days of old, I meditate on all that thou hast done; I muse on what thy hands have wrought.

6. I stretch out my hands to thee; my soul thirsts for thee like a parched land.
7. Make haste to answer me, O Lord! My spirit fails! Hide not thy face from me, lest I be like those who go down to the Pit.
8. Let me hear in the morning of thy steadfast love, for in thee I put my trust. Teach me the way I should go, for to thee I lift up my soul.
9. Deliver me, O Lord, from my enemies! I have fled to thee for refuge!
10. Teach me to do thy will, for thou art my God! Let thy good spirit lead me on a level path!
11. For thy name's sake, O Lord, preserve my life! In thy righteousness bring me out of trouble!
12. And in thy steadfast love cut off my enemies, and destroy all my adversaries, for I am thy servant.

FOURTH SUNDAY IN LENT

Psalm 147

1. Praise the Lord! For it is good to sing praises to our God; for he is gracious, and a song of praise is seemly.
2. The Lord builds up Jerusalem; he gathers the outcasts of Israel.
3. He heals the brokenhearted, and binds up their wounds.
4. He determines the number of the stars, he gives to all of them their names.
5. Great is our Lord, and abundant in power; his understanding is beyond measure.
6. The Lord lifts up the downtrodden, he casts the wicked to the ground.
7. Sing to the Lord with thanksgiving; make melody to our God upon the lyre!
8. He covers the heavens with clouds, he prepares rain for the earth, he makes grass grow upon the hills.
9. He gives to the beasts their food, and to the young ravens which cry.
10. His delight is not in the strength of the horse, nor his pleasure in the legs of a man;
11. But the Lord takes pleasure in those who fear him, in those who hope in his steadfast love.
12. Praise the Lord, O Jerusalem! Praise your God, O Zion!
13. For he strengthens the bars of your gates; he blesses your sons within you.
14. He makes peace in your borders; he fills you with the finest of the wheat.
15. He sends forth his command to the earth; his word runs swiftly.
16. He gives snow like wool; he scatters hoarfrost like ashes.
17. He casts forth his ice like morsels; who can stand before his cold?
18. He sends forth his word, and melts them; he makes his wind blow, and the waters flow.
19. He declares his word to Jacob, his statutes and ordinances to Israel.
20. He has not dealt thus with any other nation; they do not know his ordinances. Praise the Lord!

FIFTH SUNDAY IN LENT

Psalm 51

1. Have mercy on me, O God, according to thy steadfast love; according to thy abundant mercy blot out my transgressions.
2. Wash me thoroughly from my iniquity, and cleanse me from my sin!
3. For I know my transgressions, and my sin is ever before me.
4. Against thee, thee only, have I sinned, and done that which is evil in thy sight, so that thou art justified in thy sentence and blameless in thy judgment.
5. Behold, I was brought forth in iniquity, and in sin did my mother conceive me.
6. Behold, thou desirest truth in the inward being; therefore teach me wisdom in my secret heart.
7. Purge me with hyssop, and I shall be clean; wash me, and I shall be whiter than snow.
8. Fill me with joy and gladness; let the bones which thou hast broken rejoice.
9. Hide thy face from my sins, and blot out all my iniquities.
10. Create in me a clean heart, O God, and put a new and right spirit within me.
11. Cast me not away from thy presence, and take not thy holy Spirit from me.
12. Restore to me the joy of thy salvation, and uphold me with a willing spirit.
13. Then I will teach transgressors thy ways, and sinners will return to thee.
14. Deliver me from bloodguiltiness, O God, thou God of my salvation, and my tongue will sing aloud of thy deliverance.
15. O Lord, open thou my lips, and my mouth shall show forth thy praise.
16. For thou hast no delight in sacrifice; were I to give a burnt offering, thou wouldst not be pleased.
17. The sacrifice acceptable to God is a broken spirit; a broken and contrite heart, O God, thou wilt not despise.
18. Do good to Zion in thy good pleasure; rebuild the walls of Jerusalem, then wilt thou delight in right sacrifices, in burnt offerings and whole burnt offerings; then bulls will be offered on thy altar.

PALM SUNDAY

Psalm 24

1. The earth is the Lord's and the fulness thereof, the world and those who dwell therein;
2. For he has founded it upon the seas, and established it upon the rivers.
3. Who shall ascend the hill of the Lord? And who shall stand in his holy place?
4. He who has clean hands and a pure heart, who does not lift up his soul to what is false, and does not swear deceitfully.

5. He will receive blessing from the Lord, and vindication from the God of his salvation.

6. Such is the generation of those who seek him, who seek the face of the God of Jacob.

7. Lift up your heads, O gates! and be lifted up, O ancient doors! that the King of glory may come in.

8. Who is the King of glory? The Lord, strong and mighty, the Lord, mighty in battle!

9. Lift up your heads, O gates! and be lifted up, O ancient doors; that the King of glory may come in.

10. Who is this King of glory? The Lord of hosts, he is the King of Glory!

MONDAY BEFORE EASTER

Psalm 71

1. In thee, O Lord, do I take refuge; let me never be put to shame!

2. In thy righteousness deliver me and rescue me; incline thy ear to me, and save me!

3. Be thou to me a rock of refuge, a strong fortress, to save me, for thou art my rock and my fortress.

4. Rescue me, O my God, from the hand of the wicked, from the grasp of the unjust and cruel man.

5. For thou, O Lord, art my hope, my trust, O Lord, from my youth.

6. Upon thee I have leaned from my birth; thou art he who took me from my mother's womb. My praise is continually to thee.

7. I have been as a portent to many; but thou art my strong refuge.

8. My mouth is filled with thy praise, and with thy glory all the day.

9. Do not cast me off in the time of old age; forsake me not when my strength is spent.

10. For my enemies speak concerning me, those who watch for my life consult together, and say,

11. "God has forsaken him; pursue and seize him, for there is none to deliver him."

12. O God, be not far from me; O my God, make haste to help me!

13. May my accusers be put to shame and consumed; with scorn and disgrace may they be covered who seek my hurt.

14. But I will hope continually, and will praise thee yet more and more.

15. My mouth will tell of thy righteous acts, of thy deeds of salvation all the day, for their number is past my knowledge.

16. With the mighty deeds of the Lord God I will come, I will praise thy righteousness, thine alone.

17. O God, from my youth thou hast taught me, and I still proclaim thy wondrous deeds.

18. So even to old age and gray hairs, O God, do not forsake me, till I proclaim thy might to all the generations to come.

19. Thy power and thy righteousness, O God, reach the high heavens. Thou who hast done great things, O God, who is like thee?

20. Thou who hast made me see many sore troubles wilt revive me again; from the depths of the earth thou wilt bring me up again.

21. Thou wilt increase my honor, and comfort me again.

22. I will also praise thee with the harp for thy faithfulness, O my God; I will sing praises to thee with the lyre, O Holy One of Israel.

23. My lips will shout for joy, when I sing praises to thee; my soul also, which thou hast rescued.

24. And my tongue will talk of thy righteous help all the day long, for they have been put to shame and disgrace who sought to do me hurt.

TUESDAY BEFORE EASTER

Psalm 6

1. O Lord, rebuke me not in thy anger, nor chasten me in thy wrath.

2. Be gracious to me, O Lord, for I am languishing; O Lord, heal me, for my bones are troubled.

3. My soul also is sorely troubled. But thou, O Lord—how long?

4. Turn, O Lord, save my life; deliver me for the sake of thy steadfast love.

5. For in death there is no remembrance of thee; in Sheol who can give thee praise?

6. I am weary with my moaning; every night I flood my bed with tears; I drench my couch with my weeping.

7. My eye wastes away because of grief, it grows weak because of all my foes.

8. Depart from me, all you workers of evil; for the Lord has heard the sound of my weeping.

9. The Lord has heard my supplication; the Lord accepts my prayer.

10. All my enemies shall be ashamed and sorely troubled; they shall turn back, and be put to shame in a moment.

WEDNESDAY BEFORE EASTER

Psalm 94

1. O Lord, thou God of vengeance, thou God of vengeance, shine forth!

2. Rise up, O judge of the earth; render to the proud their deserts!

3. O Lord, how long shall the wicked, how long shall the wicked exult?

4. They pour out their arrogant words, they boast, all the evildoers.

5. They crush thy people, O Lord, and afflict thy heritage.

6. They slay the widow and the sojourner, and murder the fatherless;

7. And they say, "The Lord does not see; the God of Jacob does not perceive."

8. Understand, O dullest of the people! Fools, when will you be wise?

9. He who planted the ear, does he not hear? He who formed the eye, does he not see?

10. He who chastens the nations, does he not chastise? He who teaches men knowledge,

11. The Lord, knows the thoughts of man, that they are but a breath.

12. Blessed is the man whom thou dost chasten, O Lord, and whom thou dost teach out of thy law

13. To give him respite from days of trouble, until a pit is dug for the wicked.

14. For the Lord will not forsake his people; he will not abandon his heritage;
15. For justice will return to the righteous, and all the upright in heart will follow it.
16. Who rises up for me against the wicked? Who stands up for me against evildoers?
17. If the Lord had not been my help, my soul would soon have dwelt in the land of silence.
18. When I thought, "My foot slips," thy steadfast love, O Lord, held me up.
19. When the cares of my heart are many, thy consolations cheer my soul.
20. Can wicked rulers be allied with thee, who frame mischief by statute?
21. They band together against the life of the righteous, and condemn the innocent to death.
22. But the Lord has become my stronghold, and my God the rock of my refuge.
23. He will bring back on them their iniquity and wipe them out for their wickedness; the Lord our God will wipe them out.

MAUNDY THURSDAY
Psalm 116

1. I love the Lord, because he has heard my voice and my supplications.
2. Because he inclined his ear to me, therefore I will call on him as long as I live.
3. The snares of death encompassed me; the pangs of Sheol laid hold on me; I suffered distress and anguish.
4. Then I called on the name of the Lord: "O Lord, I beseech thee, save my life!"
5. Gracious is the Lord, and righteous; our God is merciful.
6. The Lord preserves the simple; when I was brought low, he saved me.
7. Return, O my soul, to your rest; for the Lord has dealt bountifully with you.
8. For thou hast delivered my soul from death, my eyes from tears, my feet from stumbling;
9. I walk before the Lord in the land of the living.
10. I kept my faith, even when I said, "I am greatly afflicted";
11. I said in my consternation, "Men are all a vain hope."
12. What shall I render to the Lord for all his bounty to me?
13. I will lift up the cup of salvation and call on the name of the Lord,
14. I will pay my vows to the Lord in the presence of all his people.
15. Precious in the sight of the Lord is the death of his saints.
16. O Lord, I am thy servant; I am thy servant, the son of thy handmaid. Thou hast loosed my bonds.
17. I will offer to thee the sacrifice of thanksgiving and call on the name of the Lord.
18. I will pay my vows to the Lord in the presence of all his people,
19. In the courts of the house of the Lord, in your midst, O Jerusalem. Praise the Lord!

GOOD FRIDAY

Psalm 22

1. My God, my God, why hast thou forsaken me? Why art thou so far from helping me, from the words of my groaning?

2. O my God, I cry by day, but thou dost not answer; and by night, but find no rest.

3. Yet thou art holy, enthroned on the praises of Israel.

4. In thee our fathers trusted, and thou didst deliver them.

5. To thee they cried, and were saved; in thee they trusted, and were not disappointed.

6. But I am a worm, and no man; scorned by men, and despised by the people.

7. All who see me mock at me, they make mouths at me, they wag their heads;

8. "He committed his cause to the Lord; let him deliver him, let him rescue him, for he delights in him!"

9. Yet thou art he who took me from the womb; thou didst keep me safe upon my mother's breasts.

10. Upon thee was I cast from my birth, and since my mother bore me thou hast been my God.

11. Be not far from me, for trouble is near and there is none to help.

12. Many bulls encompass me, strong bulls of Bashan surround me;

13. They open wide their mouths at me, like a ravening and roaring lion.

14. I am poured out like water, and all my bones are out of joint; my heart is like wax, it is melted within my breast;

15. My strength is dried up like a potsherd, and my tongue cleaves to my jaws; thou dost lay me in the dust of death.

16. Yea, dogs are round about me; a company of evildoers encircle me; they have pierced my hands and feet—

17. I can count all my bones—they stare and gloat over me;

18. They divide my garments among them, and for my raiment they cast lots.

19. But thou, O Lord, be not far off! O thou my help, hasten to my aid!

20. Deliver my soul from the sword, my life from the power of the dog!

21. Save me from the mouth of the lion, my afflicted soul from the horns of the wild oxen!

22. I will tell of thy name to my brethren; in the midst of the congregation I will praise thee:

23. You who fear the Lord, praise him! all you sons of Jacob, glorify him, and stand in awe of him, all you sons of Israel!

24. From thee comes my praise in the great congregation; my vows I will pay before those who fear him.

25. For he has not despised or abhorred the affliction of the afflicted; and he has not hid his face from him, but has heard, when he cried to him.

26. The afflicted shall eat and be satisfied; those who seek him shall praise the Lord! May your hearts live for ever!

27. All the ends of the earth shall remember and turn to the Lord; and all the families of the nations shall worship before him.

28. For dominion belongs to the Lord, and he rules over the nations.

29. Yea, to him shall all the proud of the earth bow down; before him shall bow all who go down to the dust, and he who cannot keep himself alive.

30. Posterity shall serve him; men shall tell of the Lord to the coming generation, and proclaim his deliverance to a people yet unborn, that he has wrought it.

EASTER DAY

Psalms 93, 111

1. The Lord reigns; he is robed in majesty; the Lord is robed, he is girded with strength. Yea, the world is established; it shall never be moved;

2. Thy throne is established from of old; thou art from everlasting.

3. The floods have lifted up, O Lord, the floods have lifted up, O Lord, the floods have lifted up their voice, the floods lift up their roaring.

4. Mightier than the thunders of many waters, mightier than the waves of the sea, the Lord on high is mighty! Thy decrees are very sure; holiness befits thy house, O Lord, for evermore.

1. Praise the Lord. I will give thanks to the Lord with my whole heart, in the company of the upright, in the congregation.

2. Great are the words of the Lord, studied by all who have pleasure in them.

3. Full of honor and majesty is his work, and his righteousness endures for ever.

4. He has caused his wonderful works to be remembered; the Lord is gracious and merciful.

5. He provides food for those who fear him; he is ever mindful of his covenant.

6. He has shown his people the power of his works, in giving them the heritage of the nations.

7. The works of his hands are faithful and just; all his precepts are trustworthy,

8. They are established for ever and ever, to be performed with faithfulness and uprightness.

9. He sent redemption to his people; he has commanded his covenant for ever. Holy and terrible is his name!

10. The fear of the Lord is the beginning of wisdom; a good understanding have all those who practice it. His praise endures for ever!

FIRST SUNDAY AFTER EASTER

Psalm 66

1. Make a joyful noise to God, all the earth;

2. Sing the glory of his name; give to him glorious praise!

3. Say to God, "How terrible are thy deeds! So great is thy power that thy enemies cringe before thee.

4. All the earth worships thee; they sing praises to thee, sing praises to thy name."

5. Come and see what God has done: he is terrible in his deeds among men.

6. He turned the sea into dry land; men passed through the river on foot. There did we rejoice in him,

7. Who rules by his might for ever, whose eyes keep watch on the nations—let not the rebellious exalt themselves.

8. Bless our God, O peoples, let the sound of his praise be heard,

9. Who has kept us among the living, and has not let our feet slip.

10. For thou, O God, hast tested us; thou hast tried us as silver is tried.

11. Thou didst let men ride over our heads; we went through fire and through water; yet thou hast brought us forth to a spacious place.

13. I will come into thy house with burnt offerings; I will pay thee my vows,

14. That which my lips uttered and my mouth promised when I was in trouble.

15. I will offer to thee burnt offerings of fatlings, with the smoke of the sacrifice of rams; I will make an offering of bulls and goats.

16. Come and hear, all you who fear God, and I will tell what he has done for me.

17. I cry aloud to him, and he was extolled with my tongue.

18. If I had cherished iniquity in my heart, the Lord would not have listened.

19. But truly God has listened; he has given heed to the voice of my prayer.

20. Blessed by God, because he has not rejected my prayer or removed his steadfast love from me!

SECOND SUNDAY AFTER EASTER

Psalm 34:1-14

1. I will bless the Lord at all times; his praise shall continually be in my mouth.

2. My soul makes its boast in the Lord; let the afflicted hear and be glad.

3. O magnify the Lord with me, and let us exalt his name together!

4. I sought the Lord, and he answered me, and delivered me from all my fears.

5. Look to him, and be radiant; so your faces shall never be ashamed.

6. This poor man cried, and the Lord heard him, and saved him out of all his troubles.

7. The angel of the Lord encamps around those who fear him, and delivers them.

8. O taste and see that the Lord is good! Happy is the man who takes refuge in him!

9. O fear the Lord, you his saints, for those who fear him have no want!

10. The young lions suffer want and hunger; but those who seek the Lord lack no good thing.

11. Come O sons, listen to me, I will teach you the fear of the Lord.

12. What man is there who desires life, and covets many days, that he may enjoy good?

13. Keep your tongue from evil, and your lips from speaking deceit.

14. Depart from evil, and do good; seek peace, and pursue it.

THIRD SUNDAY AFTER EASTER

Psalm 113

1. Praise the Lord! Praise, O servants of the Lord, praise the name of the Lord!
2. Blessed be the name of the Lord from this time forth and for evermore!
3. From the rising of the sun to its setting the name of the Lord is to be praised!
4. The Lord is high above all nations, and his glory above the heavens!
5. Who is like the Lord our God, who is seated on high,
6. Who looks far down upon the heavens and the earth?
7. He raises the poor from the dust, and lifts the needy from the ash heap,
8. To make them sit with princes, with the princes of his people. He gives the barren woman a home, making her the joyous mother of children. Praise the Lord!

FOURTH SUNDAY AFTER EASTER

Psalm 107:1-16

1. O give thanks to the Lord, for he is good; for his steadfast love endures for ever!
2. Let the redeemed of the Lord say so, whom he has redeemed from trouble
3. And gathered in from the land, from the east and from the west, from the north and from the south.
4. Some wandered in desert wastes, finding no way to a city to dwell in;
5. Hungry and thirsty, their soul fainted within them.
6. Then thy cried to the Lord in their trouble, and he delivered them from their distress;
7. He led them by a straight way, till they reached a city to dwell in.
8. Let them thank the Lord for his steadfast love, for his wonderful works to the sons of men!
9. For he satisfies him who is thirsty, and the hungry he fills with good things.
10. Some sat in darkness and in gloom, prisoners in affliction and in irons,
11. For they had rebelled against the words of God, and spurned the counsel of the Most High.
12. Their hearts were bowed down with hard labor; they fell down, with none to help.
13. Then they cried to the Lord in their trouble, and he delivered them from their distress;
14. He brought them out of darkness and gloom, and broke their bonds asunder.
15. Let them thank the Lord for his steadfast love, for his wonderful works to the sons of men!
16. For he shatters the doors of bronze, and cuts in two the bars of iron.

FIFTH SUNDAY AFTER EASTER

Psalm 67

1. May God be gracious to us and bless us and make his face to shine upon us,

2. That thy way may be known upon earth, the saving power among all nations.

3. Let the peoples praise thee, O God; let all the peoples praise thee!

4. Let the nations be glad and sing for joy, for thou dost judge the peoples with equity and guide the nations upon earth.

5. Let the peoples praise thee, O God; let all the peoples praise thee!

6. The earth has yielded its increase; God, our God, has blessed us. God has blessed us; let all the ends of the earth fear him!

SIXTH SUNDAY AFTER EASTER

Psalm 72

1. Give the king thy justice, O God, and thy righteousness to the royal son!

2. May he judge thy people with righteousness, and thy poor with justice!

3. Let the mountains bear prosperity for the people, and the hills, in righteousness!

4. May he defend the cause of the poor of the people, give deliverance to the needy, and crush the oppressor!

5. May he live while the sun endures, and as long as the moon, throughout all generations!

6. May he be like rain that falls on the mown grass, like showers that water the earth!

7. In his days may righteousness flourish, and peace abound, will the moon be no more!

8. May he have dominion from sea to sea, and from the River to the ends of the earth!

9. May his foes bow down before him, and his enemies lick the dust!

10. May the kings of Tarshish and of the isles render him tribute, may the kings of Sheba and Seba bring gifts!

11. May all kings fall down before him, all nations serve him!

12. For he delivers the needy when he calls, the poor and him who has no helper.

13. He has pity on the weak and the needy, and saves the lives of the needy.

14. From oppression and violence he redeems their life; and precious is their blood in his sight.

15. Long may he live, may gold of Sheba be given to him! May prayer be made for him continually, and blessings invoked for him all the day!

16. May there be abundance of grain in the land; on the tops of the mountains may it wave; may its fruit be like Lebanon; and may men blossom forth from the cities like the grass of the field!

17. May his name endure for ever, his fame continue as long as the sun! May men bless themselves by him, all nations call him blessed!

18. Blessed be the Lord, the God of Israel, who alone does wondrous things.
19. Bless be his glorious name for ever; may his glory fill the whole earth! Amen and Amen!
20. The prayers of David, the son of Jesse, are ended.

WHITSUNDAY OR PENTECOST

Psalm 68:1-8

1. Let God arise, let his enemies be scattered; let those who hate him flee before him!
2. As smoke is driven away, so drive them away; as wax melts before fire, let the wicked perish before God!
3. But let the righteous be joyful; let them exult before God; let them be jubilant with joy!
4. Sing to God, sing praises to his name; lift up a song to him who rides upon the clouds; his name is the Lord, exult before him!
5. Father of the fatherless and protector of widows is God in his holy habitation.
6. God gives the desolate a home to dwell in; he leads out the prisoners to prosperity; but the rebellious dwell in a parched land.
7. O God, when thou didst go forth before thy people, when thou didst march through the wilderness,
8. The earth quaked, the heavens poured down rain, at the presence of God; you Sinai quaked at the presence of God, the God of Israel.

TRINITY SUNDAY

Psalm 33

1. Rejoice in the Lord, O you righteous! Praise befits the upright.
2. Praise the Lord with the lyre, make melody to him with the harp of ten strings!
3. Sing to him a new song, play skilfully on the strings, with loud shouts.
4. For the word of the Lord is upright; and all his work is done in faithfulness.
5. He loves righteousness and justice; the earth is full of the steadfast love of the Lord.
6. By the word of the Lord the heavens were made, and all their host by the breath of his mouth.
7. He gathered the waters of the sea as in a bottle; he put the deeps in storehouses.
8. Let all the earth fear the Lord, let all the inhabitants of the world stand in awe of him!
9. For he spoke, and it came to be; he commanded, and it stood forth.
10. The Lord brings the counsel of the nations to nought; he frustrates the plans of the peoples.
11. The counsel of the Lord stands for ever, the thoughts of his heart to all generations.
12. Blessed is the nation whose God is the Lord, the people whom he has chosen as his heritage!
13. The Lord looks down from heaven, he sees all the sons of men;

14. From where he sits enthroned he looks forth on all the inhabitants of the earth,

15. He who fashions the hearts of them all, and observes all their deeds.

16. A king is not saved by his great army; a warrior is not delivered by his great strength.

17. The war horse is a vain hope for victory, and by its great might it cannot save.

18. Behold, the eye of the Lord is on those who fear him, on those who hope in his steadfast love,

19. That he may deliver their soul from death, and keep them alive in famine.

20. Our soul waits for the Lord; he is our help and shield.

21. Yea, our heart is glad in him, because we trust in his holy name.

22. Let thy steadfast love, O Lord, be upon us, even as we hope in thee.

SECOND SUNDAY AFTER PENTECOST

Psalm 73

1. Truly God is good to the upright, to those who are pure in heart.

2. But as for me, my feet had almost stumbled, my steps had well nigh slipped.

3. For I was envious of the arrogant, when I saw the prosperity of the wicked.

4. For they have no pangs; their bodies are sound and sleek.

5. They are not in trouble as other men are; they are not stricken like other men.

6. Therefore pride is their necklace; violence covers them as a garment.

7. Their eyes swell out with fatness, their hearts overflow with follies.

8. They scoff and speak with malice; loftily they threaten oppression.

9. They set their mouths against the heavens, and their tongue struts through the earth.

10. Therefore the people turn and praise them; and find no fault in them.

11. And they say, "How can God know? Is there knowledge in the Most High?"

12. Behold, these are the wicked; always at ease, they increase in riches.

13. All in vain have I kept my heart clean and washed my hands in innocence.

14. For all the day long I have been stricken, and chastened every morning.

15. If I had said, "I will speak thus," I would have been untrue to the generation of thy children.

16. But when I thought how to understand this, it seemed to me a wearisome task,

17. Until I went into the sanctuary of God; then I perceived their end.

18. Truly thou dost set them in slippery places; thou dost make them fall to ruin.

19. How they are destroyed in a moment, swept away utterly by terrors!

20. They are like a dream when one awakes, on awaking you despise their phantoms.

21. When my soul was embittered, when I was pricked in heart,

22. I was stupid and ignorant, I was like a beast toward thee.

23. Nevertheless I am continually with thee; thou dost hold my right hand.

24. Thou dost guide me with thy counsel, and afterward thou wilt receive me to glory.

25. Whom have I in heaven but thee? And there is nothing upon earth that I desire besides thee.

26. My flesh and my heart may fail, but God is the strength of my heart and my portion for ever.

27. For lo, those who are far from thee shall perish; thou dost put an end to those who are false to thee.

28. But for me it is good to be near God; I have made the Lord God my refuge, that I may tell of all thy works.

THIRD SUNDAY AFTER PENTECOST

Psalm 15

1. O Lord, who shall sojourn in thy tent? Who shall swell on thy holy hill?

2. He who walks blamelessly, and does what is right, and speaks truth from his heart;

3. Who does not slander with his tongue, and does no evil to his friend, nor takes up a reproach against his neighbor;

4. In whose eyes a reprobate is despised, but who honors those who fear the Lord; who swears to his own hurt and does not change;

5. Who does not put out his money at interest, and does not take a bribe against the innocent.

6. He who does these things shall never be moved.

FOURTH SUNDAY AFTER PENTECOST

Psalm 11

1. In the Lord I take refuge; how can you say to me, "Flee like a bird to the mountains;

2. For lo, the wicked bend the bow, they have fitted their arrow to the string, to shoot in the dark at the upright in heart;

3. If the foundations are destroyed, what can the righteous do"?

4. The Lord is in his holy temple, the Lord's throne is in heaven; his eyes behold, his eyelids test, the children of men.

5. The Lord tests the righteous and the wicked, and his soul hates him that loves violence.

6. On the wicked he will rain coals of fire and brimstone; a scorching wind shall be the portion of their cup. For the Lord is righteous, he loves righteous deeds; the upright shall behold his face.

FIFTH SUNDAY AFTER PENTECOST

Psalm 82

1. God has taken his place in the divine council; in the midst of the gods he holds judgment:

2. "How long will you judge unjustly and show partiality to the wicked?
3. Give justice to the weak and the fatherless; maintain the right of the afflicted and the destitute.
4. Rescue the weak and the needy; deliver them from the hand of the wicked."
5. They have neither knowledge nor understanding, they walk about in darkness; all the foundations of the earth are shaken.
6. I say, "You are gods, sons of the Most High, all of you;
7. Nevertheless, you shall die like men, and fall like any prince."
8. Arise, O God, judge the earth; for to thee belong all the nations!

SIXTH SUNDAY AFTER PENTECOST

Psalm 1

1. Blessed is the man who walks not in the counsel of the wicked, nor stands in the way of sinners, nor sits in the seat of the scoffers;
2. But his delight is in the law of the Lord, and on his law he meditates day and night.
3. He is like a tree planted by streams of water, that yields its fruit in its season, and its leaf does not wither. In all that he does, he prospers.
4. The wicked are not so, but are like chaff which the wind drives away.
5. Therefore the wicked will not stand in the judgment, nor sinners in the congregation of the righteous;
6. For the Lord knows the way of the righteous, but the way of the wicked will perish.

SEVENTH SUNDAY AFTER PENTECOST

Psalm 16

1. Preserve me, O God, for in thee I take refuge.
2. I say to the Lord, "Thou art my Lord; I have no good apart from thee."
3. As for the saints in the land, they are the noble, in whom is all my delight.
4. Those who choose another god multiply their sorrows; their libations of blood I will not pour out or take their names upon my lips.
5. The Lord is my chosen portion and my cup; thou holdest my lot.
6. The lines have fallen for me in pleasant places; yea, I have a goodly heritage.
7. I bless the Lord who gives me counsel; in the right also my heart instructs me.
8. I keep the Lord always before me; because he is at my right hand, I shall not be moved.
9. Therefore my heart is glad, and my soul rejoices; my body also swells secure.
10. For thou dost not give me up to Sheol, or let thy godly one see the Pit. Thou dost show me the path of life; in thy presence there is fulness of joy, in thy right hand are pleasures for evermore.

EIGHTH SUNDAY AFTER PENTECOST

Psalm 18:1-20

1. I love thee, O Lord, my strength.
2. The Lord is my rock, and my fortress, and my deliverer, my God, my rock, in whom I take refuge, my shield, and the horn of my salvation, my stronghold.
3. I call upon the Lord, who is worthy to be praised, and I am saved from my enemies.
4. The cords of death encompassed me, the torrents of perdition assailed me;
5. The cords of Sheol entangled me, the snares of death confronted me.
6. In my distress I called upon the Lord; to my God I cried for help. From his temple he heard my voice, and my cry to him reached his ears.
7. Then the earth reeled and rocked; the foundations also of the mountains trembled and quaked, because he was angry.
8. Smoke went up from his nostrils, and devouring fire from his mouth; glowing coals flamed forth from him.
9. He bowed the heavens, and came down; thick darkness was under his feet.
10. He rode on a cherub, and flew; he came swiftly upon the wings of the wind.
11. He made darkness his covering around him, his canopy thick clouds dark with water.
12. Out of the brightness before him there broke through his clouds hailstones and coals of fire.
13. The Lord also thundered in the heavens, and the Most High uttered his voice, hailstones and coals of fire.
14. And he sent out his arrows, and scattered them; he flashed forth lightnings, and routed them.
15. Then the channels of the sea were seen, and the foundations of the world were laid bare, at thy rebuke, O Lord, at the blast of the breath of thy nostrils.
16. He reached from on high, he took me, he drew me out of many waters.
17. He delivered me from my strong enemy, and from those who hated me; for they were too mighty for me.
18. They came upon me in the day of my calamity; but the Lord was my stay.
19. He brought me forth into a broad place; he delivered me, because he delighted in me.
20. The Lord rewarded me according to my righteousness; according to the cleanness of my hands he recompensed me.

NINTH SUNDAY AFTER PENTECOST

Psalm 119:33-48

33. Teach me, O Lord, the way of thy statutes; and I will keep it to the end.
34. Give me understanding, that I may keep thy law and observe it with my whole heart.

35. Lead me in the path of thy commandments, for I delight in it.
36. Incline my heart to thy testimonies, and not to gain!
37. Turn my eyes from looking at vanities; and give me life in thy ways.
38. Confirm to thy servant thy promise, which is for those who fear thee.
39. Turn away the reproach which I dread; for thy ordinances are good.
40. Behold, I long for thy precepts; in thy righteousness give me life!
41. Let thy steadfast love come to me, O Lord, thy salvation according to thy promise;
42. Then shall I have an answer for those who taunt me, for I trust in thy word.
43. And take not the word of truth utterly out of my mouth, for my hope is in thy ordinances.
44. I will keep thy law continually, for ever and ever;
45. And I shall walk at liberty, for I have sought thy precepts.
46. I will also speak of thy testimonies before kings, and shall not be put to shame;
47. For I find my delight in thy commandments, which I love.
48. I revere thy commandments, which I love, and I will meditate on thy statutes.

TENTH SUNDAY AFTER PENTECOST

Psalm 115

1. Not to us, O Lord, not to us, but to thy name give glory, for the sake of thy steadfast love and thy faithfulness!
2. Why should the nations say, "Where is their God?"
3. Our God is in the heavens; he does whatever he pleases.
4. Their idols are silver and gold, the work of men's hands.
5. They have mouths, but do not speak; eyes, but do not see.
6. They have ears, but do not hear; noses, but do not smell.
7. They have hands, but do not feel; feet, but do not walk; and they do not make a sound in their throat.
8. Those who make them are like them; so are all who trust in them.
9. O Israel, trust in the Lord! He is their help and their shield.
10. O House of Aaron, put your trust in the Lord! He is their help and their shield.
11. You who fear the Lord, trust in the Lord! He is their help and their shield.
12. The Lord has been mindful of us; he will bless us; he will bless the house of Israel; he will bless the house of Aaron;
13. He will bless those who fear the Lord, both small and great.
14. May the Lord give you increase, you and your children!
15. May you be blessed by the Lord, who made heaven and earth!
16. The heavens are the Lord's heavens, but the earth he has given to the sons of men.
17. The dead do not praise the Lord, nor do any that go down into silence.
18. But we will bless the Lord from this time forth and for evermore. Praise the Lord!

ELEVENTH SUNDAY AFTER PENTECOST

Psalm 48

1. Great is the Lord and greatly to be praised in the city of our God!
2. His holy mountain, beautiful in elevation, is the joy of all the earth, Mount Zion, in the far north, the city of the great King.
3. Within her citadels God has shown himself a sure defense.
4. For lo, the kings assembled, they came on together.
5. As soon as they saw it, they were astounded, they were in panic, they took to flight;
6. Trembling took hold of them there, anguish as of a woman in travail.
7. By the east wind thou didst shatter the ships of Tarshish.
8. As we have heard, so have we seen in he city of the Lord of hosts, in the city of our God, which God establishes for ever.
9. We have thought on thy steadfast love, O God, in the midst of thy temple.
10. As thy name, O God, so thy praise reaches to the ends of the earth. Thy right hand is filled with victory;
11. Let Mount Zion be glad! Let the daughters of Judah rejoice because of thy judgments!
12. Walk about Zion, go round about her, number her towers,
13. Consider well her ramparts, go through citadels; that you may tell the next generation
14. That this is God, our God for ever and ever. He will be our guide for ever.

TWELFTH SUNDAY AFTER PENTECOST

Psalm 100

1. Make a joyful noise to the Lord, all the lands!
2. Serve the Lord with gladness! Come into his presence with singing!
3. Know that the Lord is God! It is he that made us, and we are his; we are his people, and the sheep of his pasture.
4. Enter his gates with thanksgiving, and his courts with praise! Give thanks to him, bless his name! For the Lord is good; his steadfast love endures for ever, and his faithfulness to all generations.

THIRTEENTH SUNDAY AFTER PENTECOST

Psalm 101

1. I will sing of loyalty and of justice; to thee, O Lord, I will sing.
2. I will give heed to the way that is blameless. Oh when wilt thou come to me? I will walk with integrity of heart within my house;
3. I will not set before my eyes anything that is base. I hate the work of those who fall away; it shall not cleave to me.
4. Perverseness of heart shall be far from me; I will know nothing of evil.
5. Him who slanders his neighbor secretly I will destroy. The man of haughty looks and arrogant heart I will not endure.
6. I will look with favor on the faithful in the land, that they may

dwell with me; he who walks in the way that is blameless shall minister to me.

7. No man who practices deceit shall dwell in my house; no man who utters lies shall continue in my presence.

8. Morning by morning I will destroy all the wicked in the land, cutting off all the evildoers from the city of the Lord.

FOURTEENTH SUNDAY AFTER PENTECOST

Psalm 42

1. As a hart longs for flowing streams, so longs my soul for thee, O God.

2. My soul thirsts for God, for the living God. When shall I come and behold the face of God?

3. My tears have been my food day and night, while men say to me continually, "Where is your God?"

4. These things I remember, as I pour out my soul: how I went with the throng, and led them in procession to the house of God, with glad shouts and songs of thanksgiving, a multitude keeping festival.

5. Why are you cast down, O my soul, and why are you disquieted within me? Hope in God; for I shall again praise him, my help and my God.

6. My soul is cast down within me, therefore I remember thee from the land of Jordan and of Hermon, from Mount Mizar.

7. Deep calls to deep at the thunder of thy cataracts; all thy waves and thy billows have gone over me.

8. By day the Lord commands his steadfast love; and at night his song is with me, a prayer to the God of my life.

9. I say to God, my rock; "Why hast thou forgotten me? Why go I mourning because of the oppression of the enemy?"

10. As with a deadly wound in my body, my adversaries taunt me, while they say to me continually, "Where is thy God?" Why are you cast down, O my soul, and why are you disquieted within me? Hope in God; for I shall again praise him, my help and my God.

FIFTEENTH SUNDAY AFTER PENTECOST

Psalm 46

1. God is our refuge and strength, a very present help in trouble.

2. Therefore we will not fear though the earth should change, though the mountains shake in the heart of the sea;

3. Though its waters roar and foam, though the mountains tremble with its tumult.

4. There is a river whose streams make glad the city of God, the holy habitation of the Most High.

5. God is in the midst of her, she shall not be moved; God will help her right early.

6. The nations rage, the kingdoms totter; he utters his voice, the earth melts.

7. The Lord of hosts is with us; the God of Jacob is our refuge.

8. Come, behold the works of the Lord, how he has wrought desolations in the earth.

9. He makes wars cease to the end of the earth; he breaks the bow, and shatters the spear, he burns the chariots with fire!

10. Be still, and know that I am God. I am exalted among the nations, I am exalted in the earth!" The Lord of hosts is with us; the God of Jacob is our refuge.

SIXTEENTH SUNDAY AFTER PENTECOST

Psalm 44

1. We have heard with our ears, O God, our fathers have told us, what deeds thou didst perform in their days, in the days of old:

2. Thou with thy own hand didst drive out the nations, but them thou didst plant; thou didst afflict the peoples, but them thou didst set free;

3. For not by their own sword did they win the land, nor did their own arm give them victory; but thy right hand, and thy arm, and the light of thy countenance; for thou didst delight in them.

4. Thou art my King and my God, who ordainest victories for Jacob.

5. Through thee we push down our foes; through thy name we tread down our assailants.

6. For not in my bow do I trust, nor can my sword save me.

7. But thou hast saved us from our foes, and hast put to confusion those who hate us.

8. In God we have boasted continually, and we will give thanks to thy name for ever.

9. Yet thou hast cast us off and abased us, and hast not gone out with our armies.

10. Thou hast made us turn back from the foe; and our enemies have gotten spoil.

11. Thou hast made us like sheep for slaughter, and hast scattered us among the nations.

12. Thou hast sold thy people for a trifle, demanding no high price for them.

13. Thou hast made us the taunt of our neighbors, the derision and scorn of those about us.

14. Thou hast made us a byword among the nations, a laughingstock among the peoples.

15. All day long my disgrace is before me, and shame has covered my face,

16. At the words of the taunters and revilers, at the sight of the enemy and the avenger.

17. All this has come upon us, though we have not forgotten thee, or been false to thy covenant.

18. Our heart has not turned back, nor have our steps departed from thy way,

19. That thou shouldst have broken us in the place of jackals, and covered us with deep darkness.

20. If we had forgotten the name of our God, or spread forth our hands to a strange god,

21. Would not God discover this? For he knows the secrets of the heart.

22. Nay, for thy sake we are slain all the day long, and accounted as sheep for the slaughter.

23. Rouse thyself! Why sleepest thou, O Lord? Awake! Do not cast us off for ever!

24. Why dost thou hide thy face? Why dost thou forget our affliction and oppression?

25. For our soul is bowed down to the dust; our body cleaves to the ground.

26. Rise up, come to our help! Deliver us for the sake of thy steadfast love!

FIRST SUNDAY IN KINGDOMTIDE

Psalm 47

1. Clap your hands, all peoples! Shout to God with loud songs of joy!

2. For the Lord, the Most High, is terrible, a great king over all the earth.

3. He subdued peoples under us, and nations under our feet.

4. He chose our heritage for us, the pride of Jacob whom he loves.

5. God has gone up with a shout, the Lord with the sound of a trumpet.

6. Sing praises to God, sing praises! Sing praises to our King, sing praises!

7. For God is the king of all the earth: sing praises with a psalm!

8. God reigns over the nations; God sits on his holy throne.

9. The princes of the peoples gather as the people of the God of Abraham.

10. For the shields of the earth belong to God; he is highly exalted!

SECOND SUNDAY IN KINGDOMTIDE

Psalm 48

1. Great is the Lord and greatly to be praised in the city of our God!

2. His holy mountain, beautiful in elevation, is the joy of all the earth, Mount Zion, in the far north, the city of the great King.

3. Within her citadels God has shown himself a sure defense.

4. For lo, the kings assembled, they came on together.

5. As soon as they saw it, they were astounded, they were in panic, they took to flight;

6. Trembling took hold of them there, anguish as of a woman in travail.

7. By the east wind thou didst shatter the ships of Tarshish.

8. As we have heard, so have we seen in the city of the Lord of hosts, in the city of our God, which God establishes for ever.

9. We have thought on thy steadfast love, O God, in the midst of thy temple.

10. As thy name, O God, so thy praise reaches to the ends of the earth. Thy right hand is filled with victory;

11. Let Mount Zion be glad! Let the daughters of Judah rejoice because of thy judgments!

12. Walk about Zion, go round about her, number her towers,

13. Consider well her ramparts, go through her citadels; that you may tell the next generation

14. That this is God, our God for ever and ever. He will be our guide for ever.

THIRD SUNDAY IN KINGDOMTIDE

Psalm 45:1-8

1. My heart overflows with a goodly theme; I address my verses to the king; my tongue is like the pen of a ready scribe.

2. You are the fairest of the sons of men; grace is poured upon your lips; therefore God has blessed you for ever.

3. Gird your sword upon your thigh, O mighty one, in your glory and majesty!

4. In your majesty ride forth victoriously for the cause of truth and to defend the right; let your right hand teach you dread deeds!

5. Your arrows are sharp in the heart of the king's enemies; the peoples fall under you.

6. Your divine throne endures for ever and ever. Your royal scepter is a scepter of equity;

7. You love righteousness and hate wickedness. Therefore God, your God, has anointed you with the oil of gladness above your fellows;

8. Your robes are all fragment with myrrh and aloes and cassia. From ivory palaces stringed instruments make you glad.

FOURTH SUNDAY IN KINGDOMTIDE

Psalm 12

1. Help, Lord; for there is no longer any that is godly; for the faithful have vanished from among the sons of men.

2. Every one utters lies to his neighbor; with flattering lips and a double heart they speak.

3. May the Lord cut off all flattering lips, the tongue that makes great boasts,

4. Those who say, "With our tongue we will prevail, our lips are with us; who is our master?"

5. "Because the poor are despoiled, because the needy groan, I will now arise," says the Lord; "I will place him in the safety for which he longs."

6. The promises of the Lord are promises that are pure, silver refined in a furnace on the ground, purified seven times.

7. Do thou, O Lord, protect us, guard us ever from this generation.

8. On every side the wicked prowl, as vileness is exalted among the sons of men.

FIFTH SUNDAY IN KINGDOMTIDE

Psalm 13

1. How long, O Lord? Wilt thou forget me for ever? How long wilt thou hide thy face from me?

2. How long must I bear pain in my soul, and have sorrow in my heart all the day? How long shall my enemy be exalted over me?

3. Consider and answer me, O Lord my God; lighten my eyes, lest I sleep the sleep of death;

4. Lest my enemy say, "I have prevailed over him"; lest my foes rejoice because I am shaken.

5. But I have trusted in thy steadfast love; my heart shall rejoice in thy salvation.
6. I will sing to the Lord, because he has dealt bountifully with me.

SIXTH SUNDAY IN KINGDOMTIDE

Psalm 4

1. Answer me when I call, O God of my right! Thou hast given me room when I was in distress. Be gracious to me, and hear my prayer.
2. O men, how long shall my honor suffer shame? How long will you love vain words, and seek after lies?
3. But know that the Lord has set apart the godly for himself; the Lord hears when I call to him.
4. Be angry, but sin not; commune with your own hearts on your beds, and be silent.
5. Offer right sacrifices, and put your trust in the Lord.
6. There are many who say, "O that we might see some good! Lift up the light of thy countenance upon us, O Lord!"
7. Thou hast put more joy in my heart than they have when their grain and wine abound.
8. In peace I will both lie down and sleep; for thou alone, O Lord, makest me dwell in safety.

SEVENTH SUNDAY IN KINGDOMTIDE

Psalm 5

1. Give ear to my word, O Lord; give heed to my groaning.
2. Hearken to the sound of my cry, my King and my God, for to thee do I pray.
3. O Lord, in the morning thou dost hear my voice; in the morning I prepare a sacrifice for thee, and watch.
4. For thou art not a God who delights in wickedness; evil may not sojourn with thee.
5. The boastful may not stand before thy eyes; thou hatest all evildoers.
6. Thou destroyest those who speak lies; the Lord abhors bloodthirsty and deceitful men.
7. But I through the abundance of thy steadfast love will enter thy house, I will worship toward thy holy temple in the fear of thee.
8. Lead me, O Lord, in thy righteousness because of my enemies; make thy way straight before me.
9. For there is no truth in their mouth; their heart is destruction, their throat is an open sepulchre, they flatter with their tongue.
10. Make them bear their guilt, O God; let them fall by their own counsels; because of their many transgressions cast them out, for they have rebelled against thee.
11. But let all who take refuge in thee rejoice, let them ever sing for joy; and do thou defend them, that those who love thy name may exult in thee.
12. For thou dost bless the righteous, O Lord; thou dost cover him with favor as with a shield.

EIGHTH SUNDAY IN KINGDOMTIDE

Psalm 3

1. O Lord, how many are my foes! Many are rising against me;
2. Many are saying of me, there is no help for him in God.
3. But thou, O Lord, art a shield about me, my glory, and the lifter of my head.
4. I cry aloud to the Lord, and he answers me from his holy hill.
5. I lie down and sleep; I wake again, for the Lord sustains me.
6. I am not afraid of ten thousands of people who have set themselves against me round about.
7. Arise, O Lord! Deliver me, O my God! For thou dost smite all my enemies on the cheek, thou dost break the teeth of the wicked.
8. Deliverance belongs to the Lord; thy blessing be upon thy people!

NINTH SUNDAY IN KINGDOMTIDE

Psalm 2

1. Why do the nations conspire, and the peoples plot in vain?
2. The kings of the earth set themselves, and the rulers take counsel together, against the Lord and his anointed, saying,
3. "Let us burst their bonds asunder, and cast their cords from us."
4. He who sits in the heavens laughs; the Lord has them in derision.
5. Then he will speak to them in his wrath, and terrify them in his fury, saying,
6. "I have set my king on Zion, my holy hill."
7. I will tell of the decree of the Lord: He said to me, "You are my son, today I have begotten you.
8. Ask of me, and I will make the nations your heritage, and the ends of the earth your possession.
9. You shall break them with a rod of iron, and dash them in pieces like a potter's vessel."
10. Now therefore, O kings, be wise; be warned, O rulers of the earth. Serve the Lord with fear, with trembling kiss his feet, lest he be angry, and you perish in the way; for his wrath is quickly kindled. Blessed are all who take refuge in him.

TENTH SUNDAY IN KINGDOMTIDE

Psalm 23

1. The Lord is my shepherd, I shall not want;
2. He makes me lie down in green pastures. He leads me beside still waters;
3. He restores my soul. He leads me in paths of righteousness for his name's sake.
4. Even though I walk through the valley of the shadow of death, I fear no evil; for thou art with me; thy rod and thy staff, they comfort me.
5. Thou preparest a table before me in the presence of my enemies; thou anointest my head with oil, my cup overflows.
6. Surely goodness and mercy shall follow me all the days of my life; and I shall dwell in the house of the Lord for ever.

ELEVENTH SUNDAY IN KINGDOMTIDE

Psalm 148

1. Praise the Lord! Praise the Lord from the heavens, praise him in the heights!
2. Praise him, all his angels, praise him, all his host!
3. Praise him, sun and moon praise him, all you shining stars!
4. Praise him, you highest heavens, and you waters above the heavens!
5. Let them praise the name of the Lord! For he commanded and they were created.
6. And he established them for ever and ever; he fixed their bounds which cannot be passed.
7. Praise the Lord from the earth, you sea monsters and all deeps,
8. Fire and hail, snow and frost, stormy wind fulfilling his command!
9. Mountains and all hills, fruit trees and all cedars!
10. Beasts and all cattle, creeping things and flying birds!
11. Kings of the earth and all peoples, princes and all rulers of the earth!
12. Young men and maidens together, old men and children!
13. Let them praise the name of the Lord, for his name alone is exalted; his glory is above earth and heaven.
14. He has raised up a horn for his people, praise for all his saints, for the people of Israel who are near to him. Praise the Lord!

TWELFTH SUNDAY IN KINGDOMTIDE

Psalm 149

1. Praise the Lord! Sing to the Lord a new song, his praise in the assembly of the faithful!
2. Let Israel be glad in his Maker, let the sons of Zion rejoice in their King!
3. Let them praise his name with dancing, making melody to him with timbrel and lyre!
4. For the Lord takes pleasure in his people; he adorns the humble with victory.
5. Let the faithful exult in glory; let them sing for joy on their couches.
6. Let the high praises of God be in their throats and two-edged swords in their hands,
7. To wreak vengeance on the nations and chastisement on the peoples,
8. To bind their kings with chains and their nobles with fetters of iron, to execute on them the judgment written! This is glory for all his faithful ones. Praise the Lord!

THIRTEENTH SUNDAY IN KINGDOMTIDE

Psalm 150

1. Praise the Lord! Praise God in his sanctuary; praise him in his mighty firmament!
2. Praise him for his mighty deed; praise him according to his exceeding greatness!
3. Praise him with trumpet sound; praise him with lute and harp!
4. Praise him with timbrel and dance; praise him with strings and pipe!

5. Praise him with sounding cymbals; praise him with loud clashing cymbals!

6. Let everything that breathes praise the Lord! Praise the Lord!

FOURTEENTH SUNDAY IN KINGDOMTIDE

Psalm 121

1. I lift up my eyes to the hills. From whence does my help come?

2. My help comes from the Lord, who made heaven and earth.

3. He will not let your foot be moved, he who keeps you will not slumber.

4. Behold, he who keeps Israel will neither slumber nor sleep.

5. The Lord is your keeper; the Lord is your shade on your right hand.

6. The sun shall not smite you by day, nor the moon by night.

7. The Lord will keep you from all evil; he will keep your life.

8. The Lord will keep your going out and your coming in from this time forth and for evermore.

THANKSGIVING SUNDAY

Psalm 147

1. Praise the Lord! For it is good to sing praises to our God; for he is gracious, and a song of praise is seemly.

2. The Lord builds up Jerusalem; he gathers the outcasts of Israel.

3. He heals the brokenhearted, and binds up their wounds.

4. He determines the number of the stars, he gives to all of them their names.

5. Great is our Lord, and abundant in power; his understanding is beyond measure.

6. The Lord lifts up the downtrodden, he casts the wicked to the ground.

7. Sing to the Lord with thanksgiving; make melody to our God upon the lyre!

8. He covers the heavens with clouds, he prepares rain for the earth, he makes grass grow upon the hills.

9. He gives to the beasts their food, and to the young ravens which cry.

10. His delight is not in the strength of the horse, nor his pleasure in the legs of the horse, nor his pleasure in the legs of a man;

11. But the Lord takes pleasure in those who fear him, in those who hope in his steadfast love.

12. Praise the Lord, O Jerusalem! Praise your God, O Zion!

13. For he strengthens the bars of your gates; he blesses your sons within you.

14. He makes peace in your borders; he fills you with the finest of the wheat.

15. He sends forth his command to the earth; his word runs swiftly.

16. He gives snow like wool; he scatters hoarfrost like ashes.

17. He casts forth his ice like morsels; who can stand before his cold?

18. He sends forth his word, and melts them; he makes his wind blow, and the waters flow.

19. He declares his word to Jacob, his statutes and ordinances to Israel.

20. He has not dealt thus with any other nation; they do not know his ordinances. Praise the Lord!

03745

Wesley, John

Prayer book; commentary by W. Maynard French

12/27/56 Mr. Roffman

$2

Current religious thought bk. c'56

shop, Oberlin, Ohio